SOUTHERN WRITERS ON WRITING

SOUTHERN WRITERS ON

Writing

EDITED BY Susan Cushman

FOREWORD BY Alan Lightman

UNIVERSITY PRESS OF MISSISSIPPI ❖ JACKSON

www.upress.state.ms.us

Designed by Peter D. Halverson

The University Press of Mississippi is a member of the Association
of University Presses.

Foreword © 2018 Alan Lightman.

Foreword by Alan Lightman. Portions excerpted from his memoir, *Screening Room: Family Room* (Pantheon, 2015).

"The Meek Shall Inherit the Memoir: Then and Now" by Harrison Scott Key. Originally published in *Creative Nonfiction Journal* 55, Spring 2015. Reprinted by permission from the author.

"In the Land of Cotton" by John M. Floyd. An early version of this essay was originally published as a blog post on the website *Criminal Brief*, February 2, 2008. Reprinted by permission of the author.

"A Life in Books" by Lee Smith. From *Dimestore: A Writer's Life* by Lee Smith, © 2016 by Lee Smith. Reprinted by permission of Algonquin Books of Chapel Hill. All rights reserved.

"Saving What Cannot Be Saved: On the Baton Rouge Floods of 2016 and My Nostalgia for the Half-Gone" by M. O. Walsh. Originally published by *Oxford American*, November 1, 2016. Reprinted by permission of the author.

First printing 2018
∞

Library of Congress Cataloging-in-Publication Data

Names: Cushman, Susan, 1951– editor. | Lightman, Alan P., 1948– writer of foreword.
Title: Southern writers on writing / edited by Susan Cushman; foreword by
    Alan Lightman.
Description: Jackson: University Press of Mississippi, 2018. | Includes index. |
Identifiers: LCCN 2017045051 (print) | LCCN 2017053055 (ebook) | ISBN
    9781496815019 (epub single) | ISBN 9781496815026 (epub institutional) |
    ISBN 9781496815033 (pdf single) | ISBN 9781496815040 (pdf institutional)
    | ISBN 9781496815002 (cloth: alk. paper)
Subjects: LCSH: American literature—Southern States—History and criticism.
    | American literature—21st century—History and criticism. | Authors,
    American—21st century. | Southern States—Intellectual life—1865– |
    Southern States—In literature
Classification: LCC PS261 (ebook) | LCC PS261 .S6174 2018 (print) | DDC
    810.9/975—dc23
LC record available at https://lccn.loc.gov/2017045051

British Library Cataloging-in-Publication Data available

Contents

II. BECOMING A *SOUTHERN* WRITER

III. PLACE, POLITICS, PEOPLE

IV. WRITING ABOUT RACE

V. ON THE CRAFT OF WRITING

VI. A LITTLE HELP FROM MY FRIENDS

Foreword

Alan Lightman

I grew up in Memphis in the roiling 1950s and 1960s, in a large and noisy family of brothers, cousins, grandparents, uncles, and aunts. For college, I left the planet called the South and never moved back. But over the decades, I've come to realize how deep the South is in my body. It's there in some ways that I'm aware of, such as my (relatively) slow speech, my flat "i's," my habit of always, always opening the door for a female. It's also there in my unconscious, like gravity, an invisible force that points to the center.

In high school, I acted in school plays as an antidote to my shyness. I remember my first drama course with Mr. Crain. For the first three or four months of the course, he did nothing but attempt to teach us how to pronounce words as northerners do. "You beasts will never make it to the stage talking like southern rednecks." He spent hours trying to exterminate our flat "i" and replace it with the high-toned and taut "i" heard in other parts of the United States of America. We had to hold our mouths open, as in a doctor's office, while he prodded our tongues and the soft tissues of our throats with a popsicle stick to show us which parts of our oral anatomy must be brought into play to correct the defective sounds. The southern "i," which I associate with the grace and gentility of the region, is a lazy exhalation of air and can be accomplished with a slack jaw, no movement of the tongue, and, in fact, no effort at all—almost like an unconscious sigh or a tiny gasp when turning over during a night's sleep. By contrast, the "i" uttered by a northerner is a high-calorie proposition requiring the lower jaw and tongue to be jerked back while air is somehow forced in reverse along the bottom of the mouth, deflected against the throat, and finally launched forward along the roof of the mouth. That, at any rate, is how it felt to a young person raised on the gentler movements of the South. Even to this day, after Mr. Crain's training and after inhabiting the upper parts of the country for fifty years, I must brace myself to come forth with a northern "i." There were numerous other sounds Mr. Crain taught us to stifle, and others we had to manufacture from scratch. We incorrectly pronounced "sure" like "shoo-ah," "barley" like "bawly," "pen" like "pin," "ruined" like "roined."

I remember small things, but telling for a writer. I remember the way that waitresses smiled at you and always gave you a second glass of iced tea. The way that Willie, a wiry black man with gold-capped front teeth who worked at the golf club, would say "Have a blessed day." The way that Blanche ironed. Blanche worked for our family for all of my childhood. (At that time, and for many years after, every white family of middle class or above could afford a black maid.) Blanche did the ironing on two days of the week. Shirts, blouses, and underwear on one day, tablecloths, sheets, and cotton napkins on the other. A huge pile of laundry waited in a couple of baskets at her feet. One by one, she would bend over and lift up each item, straighten it, pat it, and stretch it out on her ironing board as if she were about to perform an operation. Then she would dip her hand into a bowl of water and sprinkle the fabric with a quick flick of her fingers. When the hot iron met the damp fabric, it hissed and sent up a little puff of steam. Blanche had a routine. With a shirt, she would first press the front, moving the iron in a little semi-circle around each button. Then the buttonhole side, then the collar, then the sleeves in short strokes, careful not to form any double creases, and finally the back in long strokes. Her technique, slow and rhythmic, was hypnotizing to watch. Pat. Sprinkle. Back and forth. Up. Down. Turn. Pat. Sprinkle. Up. Down. Up. Down. After each shirt was done, she put it on a hanger, buttoned the top two buttons, and hung it from the door knob of the silver closet.

Years later, when I began to iron my own shirts, I was astonished to realize that I had unconsciously memorized Blanche's technique and rhythm, in the same way that my fingers learned the notes of a Chopin sonata. Pat. Sprinkle. Back and forth. Up. Down. And I can still picture Blanche standing at the ironing board softly humming a gospel song, her face moist with sweat, a fan chopping the heat, an ashtray on the table with her smoldering cigarette. Every minute or so, she would put the iron down and take a long drag from her Pall Mall.

The chapters in this book span a huge range of topics in writing, from Clyde Edgerton's tips for students of fiction writing to Lee Smith's moving and vivid personal account of her life as a writer. What all of these southern writers share is a deep immersion in the literary imagination, the desire to live many lives. It would be hard to prove that southern writers experience literature any differently than do northern or western writers, and equally hard to prove that there is anything uniquely southern about the craft of southern writers. Edgerton's tips for writing good fiction—such as the importance of arresting details or of including only one character in each paragraph—are not restricted to southern writing. Smith's wonderful invention of characters in her childhood probably happens in the playful minds of young writers all over the world. That said, anyone who has travelled the country knows that the South has a unique character and culture. That culture is absorbed in every square inch of skin of the writers who ever lived in the South, shapes their being, and can be seen in the particular stories they write. For example, the constant and sometimes burdensome heat of the South in Eudora Welty's "No Place for You My Love." The dignity and graciousness of the South in William Faulkner's "A Rose for Emily." The social order and traditions of the South in Peter Taylor's "Summons to Memphis." And if the South is not clearly evident in each of the chapters of this book, it is there between the lines, quiet, respectful but proud, unhurried, with soft rounded contours, like the southern spoken "i."

Acknowledgments

$\mathscr{S}$ir Isaac Newton once said, "If I have seen further, it is by standing on the shoulders of giants." This is certainly true of my work in putting together this anthology. In addition to the twenty-five gifted writers who contributed essays and Alan Lightman, who wrote the foreword, I drew inspiration from others who have made huge contributions to the southern canon of literature. Watch for section quotes by Rick Bragg, Pat Conroy, Maggie Britton Vaughn, Zora Neale Hurston, Flannery O'Connor, and William Faulkner.

Another "giant" I would like to thank is Lee Smith, for her inspiration. I was reading her book, *Dimestore: A Writer's Life*, when the idea came to me to put together an anthology. I loved the entire book, but chose to reprint one chapter, "A Life in Books," as an essay for *Southern Writers Writing*. When I emailed Lee to thank her, she was excited about the anthology and said she only wished she had time to write an original essay for it. Such a generous spirit.

When I began putting together my list of authors to invite to contribute essays, I quickly realized that my circle of acquaintances in this realm wasn't big enough. So I turned to my friend Neil White (*In the Sanctuary of Outcasts*), creative director of Nautilus Publishing Company in Oxford, Mississippi, for help. He immediately sent me an expanded list, which added a half dozen or more to my cadre of writers. I was humbled and grateful that these busy, accomplished folks agreed to contribute without having ever met me. I'm sure one reason for their compliance was our publisher—the next folks I want to thank for making this book possible. The University Press of Mississippi responded quickly to my query and encouraged me by their enthusiasm for the project. Since I am native of Jackson and attended the University of Mississippi, it was important to me to have this work published by them. Thanks to everyone on their staff for their help in putting together such a wonderful anthology.

I'd like to add a few words about the photograph on the cover, which was done by Oxford, Mississippi photographer, Ed Croom. Ed shot the photograph while thinking about some elements that might influence what is written by a southern writer. In Ed's words:

> *This photograph was taken at William Faulkner's Rowan Oak. The tenant house first was built for Caroline Barr or Mammy Callie who raised Faulkner and was a storyteller in her own right. Later it housed the caretakers of the four acres of cultivated land, cows and horses that Faulkner owned. The toughness of the Osage Orange is prominent in the foreground. It is an old tree native to the South and Midwest, used for shade and fence posts, knife handles, and gun stocks. The wood is hard and resists decay and the tree lives with no special care for decades. The tenant house in the background is where the generally invisible black workers lived who were said to be like family, but their home is a very different shelter than the big house in front. These workers, who mostly had only a first name, were the source of hard labor, maintaining the land and the fences, animal barns, and houses. They cleaned and cooked and reared the children of the property owners. This was true of Faulkner, too.*

To be a southerner, born or re-planted here by fate, is to drive through that stillness of landscape and spirit and *feel* it, and we mumble a few lines of a song from childhood, to gather the ghosts of our tribe around us.

—RICK BRAGG, *MY SOUTHERN JOURNEY*

Introduction

Susan Cushman

*I*n his book *A Lowcountry Heart: Reflections on a Writing Life* (published posthumously), the author Pat Conroy says: "My mother, Southern to the bone, once told me; 'All Southern literature can be summed up in these words: "On the night the hogs ate Willie, Mama died when she heard what Daddy did to Sister."'"

Southern writers know how to tell a story, and as Flannery O'Connor said, "Anybody who has survived his childhood has enough information about life to last him the rest of his days."

In *Southern Writers on Writing*, twenty-six southern authors spill their guts on the art of their craft. Why is it important that they are southern? Do I feel that we have something to prove, or just something to offer? Maybe a little of both.

A few years ago I was driving down Highway 6, which connects I-55 with Oxford, Mississippi, on my way to a Creative Nonfiction Conference I helped direct, when I saw a sign by the road that said: YES WE CAN READ. A FEW OF US CAN EVEN WRITE. The sign, which was part of the Mississippi, Believe It! campaign, showed pictures of fourteen revered writers, including Pulitzer Prize winners and other prominent authors. As I look at their names now, I realize they represent only a small number of the gifted writers the state—and the region—has produced. Growing up in Mississippi, I always felt that I had something to prove when my home state, and the South in general, came under attack by those who thought themselves superior to us in various ways.

But this book isn't just an attempt to show up the ignorance of those who would belittle the South. It's a joyous celebration of our culture and the writers who bring it to life on the page as they create a contemporary canon of southern literature. It was important to me to have diversity in this collection, which contains works by thirteen women and thirteen men, amongst whom are four African Americans and four poets. These authors hail from nine states: Mississippi, Alabama, Louisiana, Tennessee, Georgia, South Carolina, North Carolina, Virginia, and Florida. The bulk of the contributors work primarily with fiction, but several have also published nonfiction works.

Realizing that the topics overlap quite a bit, I chose to group them thematically. Jim Dees starts off the first section, "Becoming a Writer," with a candid story of learning to overcome fear—first of the high dive, and later of "flinging himself at the universe as a writer"—in his essay, "Off the Deep End." In "Consider Kudzu," Joe Formichella, who acknowledges that there is a definitive oral culture in the South, argues that being a writer is both a curse and a blessing—a "damned privilege"—so we should just get on with it and tell the story. Harrison Scott Key invites the reader to "sit in the cockpit of my soul and soar through the atmosphere of me" as he discovers the need for humility and transparency in "The Meek Shall Inherit the Memoir: Then and Now." A bookworm as a child, Cassandra King grew up with an eccentric array of characters like Wampus Kitty, Old Bloody Bones, and Aunt Fenny-Rump, but it was her great-grandfather Josiah King, a writer whom she thanks for his genes, who eventually catapulted her into fiction writing as she relates in "The Ghost of Josiah King." Corey Mesler writes about how agoraphobia informs his work ethic and spurs him to creativity even as he is chained to his desk and a solitary lifestyle in "The Agoraphobic Writer."

In Section II, "Becoming a *Southern* Writer," Patti Callahan Henry tells *why* she writes in "What Happens Next," showing us that writing gives her the power "to make a choice, to change an outcome, to project forward to what might happen next" . . . and "to allow hope to infuse some of the darker times." In "Stardust: An Essay on Voice in Four Parts," Sonja Livingston—a northern transplant—writes about how she was "won over by how exotic the southern voice sounded" at the graduate writing program she attended in New Orleans one summer, explaining how "it's not only the words we use, but their shape and sound that matter." Sally Palmer Thomason counts Maya Angelou and Willie Morris among the gifted southern authors who helped her gain a greater appreciation for her chosen homeland after leaving California for Memphis, Tennessee, in "How I Became a Southerner."

Section III, "Place, Politics, People," opens with "Southern Fiction: A Tool to Stretch the Soul and Soften the Heart," Louisiana native Julie Cantrell's love letter to her home state, saying: "The South offers a fantasy, a place where time slows and anxieties melt like the ice in a glass of sugar cane rum." In "The Burden of Southern Literature" Katherine Clark encourages southern writers not to "wallow in southern-ness," but to use the foundation laid by Faulkner and others "as a springboard launching us in the new and different directions demanded by a changing culture." The prolific mystery short story author John M. Floyd writes about the South he loves as a place of contrasts, with a rich oral history that offers much fodder for writers in "In the Land of Cotton." Jennifer Horne writes about being "geographically located in Alabama but psychologically apart from its churches on every corner, its conservative politics, its fascination with football, and its pressure to conform as it pretends to treasure its eccentrics" in "Where I Write." In "That's What *She* Said: The Sordid Business of Writing," Suzanne Hudson (and her semi alter-ego RP Saffire) give us a humorous but deadly serious look into the sometimes scary world of "traditional" publishing, choosing a different path in the end.

River Jordan schools a young girl from New York in all things southern during a chance encounter at the Nashville's Day of the Dead Tequila Festival in "Dirt, Death, and the Divine: The Roots of Southern Writing." Lee Smith reveals what she calls "the mysterious alchemy of fiction," declaring that writing fiction—living in someone else's story—healed her grief after the death of her son in her essay, "A Life in Books." In "On the Baton Rouge Floods of 2016 and My Nostalgia for the Half-Gone," M. O. Walsh muses on whether southern writers have a stronger bond with place and a greater sense of loss.

W. Ralph Eubanks leads off Section IV, "Writing about Race," discussing the deception and denial of Mississippi's history, weaving important nuggets of the past into his stories. In "The Past Is Just Another Name for Today," he tells us "we can all experience the past in the present if we are willing to go deep." In "Black Countermelodies" Ravi Howard explains about the importance of revealing the interiority of black characters and not just the "first voice" (the servitude) we often hear in their dialogue. Often wrapped in silence, these countermelodies "give the characters the distance to live and maneuver." Pulitzer Prize nominee, poet, critic, and essayist Claude Wilkinson takes us on a colorful journey to discover what makes a place seem southern in "All That 'Southern' Jazz."

In Section V, "On the Craft of Writing," novelist and nonfiction writer Clyde Edgerton brings his teaching skills to bear in his didactic essay "Three 'One Things,'" encouraging writers to use craft to make their fiction work. Niles Reddick teaches us (and his students) how to capture the essence of what is different and unique in the South—like his aunt who kept a jar of afterbirth in the refrigerator and made art from roadkill—in "Capturing the Essence of Difference." Jacqueline Allen Trimble shares her journey as a poet, teacher, southern black woman, and social justice advocate in "A Woman Explains How Learning Poetry Is Poetry and Not Magic Made Her a Poet." Although her essay would fit equally well in sections on "Race" or "Place, Politics, People," her wisdom on the importance of craft in writing speaks strongly to everyone who values the written word.

Section VI, "A Little Help from My Friends," opens with my essay "Hard Labor: The Birth of a Novelist," in which I sing the praises of early lovers who planted the seeds and midwives who helped bring them to fruition in my own writing career. Many of those people have essays in this book. Wendy Reed takes us into a world of "literary seductions" in her three-part essay "Lyrical Acts," revealing the parts beds, family, boyfriends, and *words* played in moving her to write, calling the act of writing "peeling the forbidden fruit with a nib." In "The Necessity of Writer Friends," Nicole Seitz writes about finding her tribe in a diverse writers' group that met at a local bookstore, and later connecting with another author she calls her "thin friend" because of the transparency of their spiritual bond. Mississippi author Michael Farris Smith attributes his initial inspiration to Barry Hannah and Larry Brown, and later William Gay, Richard Yates, and Harry Crews. But he shares in "Keep Truckin'" that it was ultimately perseverance and hard work that got him published.

Whether you are a writer, a reader, or just a lover of good literature and all things southern, I hope you will find something to love in this collection.

I

Becoming a Writer

Do you think that Hemingway knew he was a writer at twenty years old? No, he did not. Or Fitzgerald, or Wolfe. This is a difficult concept to grasp. Hemingway didn't know he was Ernest Hemingway when he was a young man. Faulkner didn't know he was William Faulkner. But they had to take the first step. They had to call themselves writers. That is the first revolutionary act a writer has to make. It takes courage. But it's necessary.

—PAT CONROY, *MY LOSING SEASON: A MEMOIR*

Off the Deep End

Jim Dees

The writer in America isn't a part of the culture of this country.
He's like a fine dog. People like him around, but he's of no use.
—WILLIAM FAULKNER INTERVIEW, *LION IN THE GARDEN* (1955)

*W*hat an unnatural, unseemly, urge it is to write. Who do we think we are? What part of the brain houses such a narcissistic, parasitic proclivity? Is it the same region that encourages child molesters or IRS agents? When does one "come out" to friends and family as a writer? Is there "conversion therapy" available? Just what is the deal? Or, as today's acronym-savvy kids say: WTF?

During my tender years in the harsh black-and-white days of the late 1950s–early '60s in the Mississippi Delta port city of Greenville, there were actual writers in town such as Bern Keating and Jo Haxton (who wrote under the name Ellen Douglas). They published books and enjoyed national followings and were respected in most quarters. Of course, there was the gruffer, redneck element that looked on writing as side work if not downright sissified.

Real men put on a suit and went to an office, or they drove a tractor or worked construction or at least knew how to work on cars. The old racist salts of that era would tell you that real men didn't sit and scratch words on a note pad, that's what secretaries were for.

If you tried to offer up William Faulkner as an example of writing success, this crowd would hoot you down. "That nut?! He never worked a day in his life. No 'count!"

Of course, writing goes back thousands of years. Early cave dwellers scratched primitive images on the cave walls to provide a record for succeeding cave-persons to inform them about the weather, what tools to use, and how gross the food was.

It is an enduring conundrum why Mississippi has produced so many writers. A place so impoverished, violent, and ignorant, the sentiment goes, can't possibly also be home to minds capable of great art. If you subtract Mississippi from American arts and letters, you'd still have hip hop and Stephen King but America's canon of arts would be much poorer. Who wants to live in a world without Elvis?

Taking the Mississippi category a step deeper, to my adopted hometown of Oxford, Mississippi, one finds an inordinate slice of the writing pie, anywhere from thirty to fifty nationally published authors associated with this town of twenty thousand-ish.

The Oxford list includes the current Poet Laureate of Mississippi, the author of the Spencer mystery series, two Emmy winners, an Edgar Award winner, mega-mega seller John Grisham, and the aforementioned Faulkner. Other fine artists such as Willie Morris, Larry Brown, and the inestimable Barry Hannah are all past residents who produced great work here. The last three, Hannah, Morris, and Brown, were friends and, in Willie's case, a neighbor of mine. During the 1980s in Oxford, I had a ringside seat to observe them putting it all on the line to write. Brown quit his steady job with the Oxford Fire Department to commit to his craft—even with three small children. Morris moved to Oxford and picked up his writing career in a modest faculty bungalow at Ole Miss following a turbulent tenure at *Harper's Magazine* and coming off a crippling divorce. Hannah never faltered in output while teaching full class loads. He wrote his final novel, *Yonder Stands Your Orphan*, while suffering the debilitating ravages of chemotherapy.

Of the question, "Why has Mississippi produced so many great writers?" Willie Morris theorized a very simple answer: "Sour mash and memory." I would never contradict him but it seems that one cancels out the other. Willie regaled groups of late-night listeners on a regular basis after the bars closed, at his home in Oxford. Many nights I was privileged to be part of a revolving group of midnight marauders who would gather for last call or three.

Willie had a seemingly limitless supply of tales—all brought to vivid life with his unerring recall and precise vocabulary or, failing that, more than adequate invention. He had walked the walk, been there done that, and suffered the tribulations. His writing career—the youngest ever editor at *Harper's*, the nation's oldest (some said fustiest) magazine—led him at age 32 to the absolute height of literary pinnacle in the boozy blue haze of Manhattan salons of the 1960s. There, following such southerners as author Truman Capote, broadcaster Red Smith, and *New York Times* editor Turner Catledge, among others, his much maligned southern home soil wasn't a huge barrier.

That wasn't always the case. Willie recalled that in 1956, as a Rhodes Scholar at Oxford, England (the "Other Oxford," he called it), he was assigned to pick up visiting poet, Robert Frost, at the London airport.

When Frost heard Willie's southern drawl he asked the young student where he was from. Upon hearing "Mississippi," the revered poet spat, "That's a terrible place!" Willie responded by saying the state had produced a number of worthy writers. Frost sneered, "What's the point if nobody can read?"

My hometown of Greenville had a literary pedigree thanks to the aforementioned Keating and Douglas, not to mention Hodding Carter, Walker Percy, Shelby Foote, William Alexander Percy, and Beverly Lowry, all former residents. Still, as a youngster developing a love of books stoked by our neighborhood bookmobile, the writing life seemed a distant, unattainable pipedream, like looking through the wrong end of binoculars.

My earliest literary yearnings were stirred by sports. When Bill "Whoo Hoo Mercy!" Goodrich called Ole Miss Rebel football games in the early to mid-1960s, time stood still at our house. That signature exclamation—"Whoo Hoo Mercy!"—whenever the Rebels scored or made a big play, became our catch phrase for anything fun or exciting. Even our parents used it. Seeing how Goodrich put our entire family at his, well, mercy, just through his words and sheer dint of personality, seemed to me a mysterious and heady power indeed.

One starts writing for fun and stays for the passion. It is only in a writer's later years that this vocation takes on a third dimension, as a lifeline to eternity; a way to remain on earth long after one has left it; an intruder back to the dust. Like those hairy gents in their loincloths, scratching away in their caves, writing might be viewed as a final, puny claim on immortality.

Faulkner discussed this notion in an interview: "What matters is at the end of life, when you're about to pass into oblivion, that you've at least scratched 'Kilroy was here' on the last wall of the universe." Barry Hannah agreed, telling an interviewer that writing is a way "not to be rolled over by time like a crab in the surf."

Hannah also acknowledged the scary aspects of writing, the "putting yourself out there" for all the world to see, the fear of ridicule or disparagement, or worse, cold indifference and dismissal. Regarding such fears, he had a typically Hannah-esque, to-the-jugular answer: "Fuck fear."

That's tough love, baby. It helps if you have so much fear piled on you that you break loose from sheer exhaustion of being scared. I remember, again, in those long-ago days in Greenville, the closest I ever came to experiencing domestic terrorism was swimming lessons. We had a public (of course, segregated) swimming pool at the town community center. At age six or so, they'd start you out in the shallow end with your first chopping strokes and dog paddling. This was "Beginner" class. Then, on to "Intermediate," where you began swimming laps, "freestyle"—kicking and stroking in unison while exhaling every other stroke. Looming over all this was the high diving board located over at the "deep end," separated by ropes and safety floats but it may as well have been 20,000 Leagues Under the Sea. When I dared walk over there, where the sixth-graders were diving and swimming like fish, I saw to my eternal consternation that, in the deep end, YOU COULD NOT SEE THE BOTTOM OF THE POOL.

There was no reassuring drain visible to gauge the end of the pool . . . or the world, for that matter. Gazing down through the chlorine-y waters of the deep end, my young, impressionable self imagined it was very possible that there was no bottom. Maybe you just kept swimming until you entered a point of no return and then drowned in a bottomless pit. They'd assign your dressing room basket to somebody else.

At the end of the third week, I somehow made the "Advanced" class. We were told we would be jumping off the high dive. I think the first time I walked on it, after enduring the stomach-losing ten-foot ladder to the top, I ended up lying on my stomach, inching my way toward the end like a slug. I squinted and peered over the edge, down to the blue depths in abject terror. Had someone pushed me off I would have anticipated the "Baby Ruth" scene in *Caddyshack* decades before the movie, except it wouldn't have been a Baby Ruth.

The question of that summer among my swim mates became, "Have you gone off the deep end yet?" The bravest among us steeled themselves and went for it early on. We watched as they emerged from the water with glee and got right back in line to go again. My memory, like swimming underwater with your eyes open, is blurry. I feel certain I was one of the last to go.

Finally the day arrived, the last day to finish all the qualifications to earn the "Advanced" certificate. I ascended the high dive stairs with a dry mouth and a knotted stomach. Standing on the board I felt wobbly, trying not to look down, the class seated around the pool talking and laughing, some urging me on.

I allowed myself a nanosecond of imagining myself waving it off and climbing down the stairs in disgrace. No way, baby. Not this time. I eased out to the end of the board careful to walk lighter as I went. The board dipped deeper the further out I moved, putting more spring in my step than I wanted. Out on the end, a deep breath then . . . a step into air . . . dropping, the opposite of soaring.

Jumping off the low board was pretty quick work. This high dive, closer to God, allowed for a moment of suspended animation, like entering a womb of air. A quick look down at my brave feet and then brace for impact.

Torque and bubbles accompanied me straight down into water depths I had never been before like Mike Nelson, my TV hero from the series *Sea Hunt*. Then, almost hysterical flapping to get to the surface quickly. I had busted my high dive cherry and had trouble gauging the distance or fathoming the fathoms. I broke the surface to a smattering of applause, my death-defying feat barely registering amid the cackle and chatter of boisterous school kids at the pool on a summer day. I had a bright, shiny new answer to the question, "Have you gone off the deep end yet?"

Writing involves much the same mechanics. In gathering the courage to attempt to write and then, even more daunting, to attempt to get published, one musters mojo from whatever sources, be it Barry Hannah or Mike Nelson—who was played, by the way, by the great Lloyd Bridges, who, among his many skills, had great hair underwater. Some might know him as the father of actor Jeff Bridges.

My recent book, *The Statue and the Fury*, is a true story that I had saved up for twenty years. The book covers a year in Oxford (1997) when I was a green-as-grass reporter, and a statue of William Faulkner set off a yearlong controversy involving trees versus development, and eventually the Rebel flag and racial altercations. I kept boxes of interviews and research from that year stored in my garage, assured it would make a cool book.

And then I started writing it. It was great until the second sentence.

I knew the story, even knew how I wanted to lay it out and in what order. But once I started writing it, a deadly realization seeped into my being: "Dude, you ain't a writer. Who the fuck are you kidding?" I had written newspaper columns and shorter essays for twenty years but this was a sprawling new world. I had carried this story around like a tattered phone number of an ex-girlfriend. Once I committed to starting it and finishing it, the tale quickly lost the luster and sheen it had had in my mind.

I felt relief and vindication when I came across an interview in the *Oxford American* (Fall 2001) with my go-to man, Barry Hannah. Apparently even a master like Hannah felt writer's remorse:

> Every book I've written I can't bear to read. I open the pages, and they just seem like they're about fifteen degrees below what I intended. You've just got to get over the fact what you write is going to be imperfect. You've got that dream, that gem-like flame you want to apply to something you've seen or something that's been in your heart a long time, and the first sentence murders it. It's not going to be quite what you wanted. It breaks your heart a little. I understand that Muslims would put a deliberate imperfection into the pictures they created because only God was perfect. Well, I don't have that trouble.

God bless you Barry Hannah, prose astronaut. And also the brilliant and perceptive Willie Morris and luminous Ellen Douglas and every ballsy soul who checks "writer" in the "Occupation" box. It is a cosmic ride to fling yourself at the universe as a writer and a miracle to maintain it. Maybe it starts in a bookmobile and ends at a solitary desk in a small room where, if you're lucky, the only sound heard is a keyboard.

It takes insane courage to assemble your thoughts and true deep matters of your heart and present them to a world of disdaining strangers. It is trusting in fate of the highest order to gut check yourself enough to walk the plank and take the ultimate plunge.

When people ask me what I do, I often see that old diving board while thinking, "Well, I don't wear a suit and count beans or work construction. I don't make widgets. Just what the hell do I do?"

Then I take the plunge. "I'm a writer," I say, marveling at the words every time.

Consider Kudzu

Joe Formichella

George Orwell wrote over eighty years ago—before television, remember, much less computers, radio just maturing and writing still preeminent—in "Why I Write" that, "From a very early age, perhaps the age of five or six, I knew that when I grew up I should be a writer." One of the curiouser and curiouser aspects of that statement, for me, is that as much as he professes to have known from such an early age that he "should be a writer" it's quite clear that he also knew that the prospects of actually seeing those words in print were dismal, at best. The stories of suppression and censorship, not to mention rejection, are famous, or should be: T. S. Eliot turned down *Animal Farm*, Victor Gollancz *1984*, both books that are still, and probably always will be, required reading in English speaking high schools everywhere. And those are, arguably, Orwell's *best* work. In retrospect, one might wonder, writers especially, why did he do it? Why did he subject himself to that kind of ardor, a Sisyphean task, if ever, so much subjective anguish with so little objective promise? The answer has to be simple, an Occam's Razor, Willie Sutton kind of answer: He couldn't *not* do it. Even if he tried. "Between the ages of about seventeen and twenty-four I tried to abandon this idea, but I did so with the consciousness that I was outraging my true nature and that sooner or later I should have to settle down and write books." He couldn't *not* write.

In a perfect world, that'd be the end of it, no need for further discussion, case closed. It was simple: He couldn't not write, so he did. And yet, there he was, at the threshold of hospital where the disease that would claim his brief life in a few short years was first diagnosed, *explicating* "Why I Write," suggesting, perhaps, that he'd never really come to grips with it all, and while

9

his lungs were still providing some oxygen to his brain, grappling with it anew. That's hardly surprising, and not nearly unique, I submit. Orwell just seems like a most appropriate example in these days where he's being quoted everywhere, canonized as a prophet or censored all over again. I see it in a lot of writers, from the interviews of the famous to the manuscripts of the less so, from Flannery O'Connor trying to convince us that there's hope at the core of her writing to a first-time novelist who buried the lead that would garner him a six-figure advance on a two-book New York publishing contract eight pages in, that irreconcilable impulse to somehow explain your existence, defend your choices, or excuse your work, offering a *reason* why you write, with or without challenge, if only for yourself. Maybe you should stop that. Accept that it's simple, really, Orwellian (and isn't that enough, honestly, to render this proposal agreeable: who *doesn't* thrill to the notion of "getting Orwellian" on their asses?). The truth is, you write because you can't not write. And, in keeping with right and proper scientific method, the corollary is also true: If you *can* not write, you probably should.

It's like kudzu. There's always another level to the story, another angle, another layer. Clearly, Orwell doesn't speak for all writers, even when he says something like, "All writers are vain, selfish, and lazy, and at the very bottom of their motives there lies a mystery. Writing a book is a horrible, exhausting struggle, like a long bout of some painful illness. One would never undertake such a thing if one were not driven on by some demon whom one can neither resist nor understand." William Styron told the *Paris Review* a few years later, when asked if he enjoyed writing, "I certainly don't," and after some explication suggests, "Let's face it, writing is hell." But then not more than a breath later, says, "I find that I'm simply the happiest, the placidest, when I'm writing." Malcolm Cowley *tried* to resolve the contradiction: "Not writing is the genuine hell for Styron and others in his predicament; writing at worst a purgatory," which is interesting, but probably otherwise useless. Why bother the examination? Why not, rather—without tracing too many of those doltish dozen steps—admit it, accept it, whichever, and get on with the story? Isn't that the prime motivator, after all, to tell a story, to tug on a sleeve, bend an ear, whisper, "Listen to this . . ."? Isn't the so-called writer's "predicament" as reductive as, according to John Irving, "putting black on white"? And when you consider, as Irving continues—which is no great surprise, is it?—that the stories themselves are everywhere, have all existed before the writer, *predicate* the writer, who then is no more than, "the lucky slob who found it," doesn't the whole notion that there's something like a "predicament" at all dissolve pretty quickly? To be perfectly blunt—because writing, perhaps alone in this, of all sentient endeavors, where motive and *modus* are one and the same thing, the *recipe* of the act, the story—the answer is, again, ridiculously simple: Just get on with it, tell the story. Sure, it's a curse, but it's also a blessing, a damned privilege, might be one way to look at it. Or, as John Hersey said, "Writing is the only reward."

Which brings me back to kudzu, because, after all, this is supposed to be "Southern Writers on Writing." Have to admit that I struggled with that task, on a couple of levels: that appellation, *southern writers,* foremost, followed pretty quickly by the tired old argument whether there even is such a thing, or whether it matters anymore. But because I'm probably guilty of at least two of the three character blemishes Orwell cites, I'll try to address them all at once. As an interloper—which, in the "good ol' days" would have been called a carpetbagger—I believe I have a unique perspective on the subject. If you spend any time in the South you'll notice, I noticed, these people *love* to tell stories. Now, before you get all dismissive and start turning pages for the next essay, consider the southern penchant for telling stories as akin to the Gambini existential thrill of arguing in *My Cousin Vinny.* People don't answer, or even ask a question that couldn't be considered a story. People don't give you directions, a recipe, advice, condolences, or caution. They tell you a story. Before I ever ventured below the Mason-Dixon, I had an older brother tell me that he couldn't ever live in the South, for fear he'd starve to death. On a visit to a high school friend stationed near Myrtle Beach, trying to order some dessert, he first had to hear the history of its origin, a cautionary tale about its proper pronunciation, a dissertation about the preferred method of eating it, "When all I wanted was a goddamned piece of pecan pie!" I'm not saying that's any kind of exclusive distinction, obviously. I mean, hell, oral traditions are as old as tongues themselves, from the ancients to the natives to hop-hop. I'm just saying it seems to me there's a definitive oral culture here that I've never noticed anywhere else, not in New York, certainly, and not through time spent in a border state at College Park, the Rocky Mountains, not even in Asia. Does that mean similar cultures don't exist elsewhere? Of course not. I just didn't *notice* them. That could easily be because I wasn't paying the necessary attention, easily, but I don't really think so. Still, I wondered about it, oftentimes out loud. Most of the time those inquiries were met with just a disinterested shrug, as if to say, "Yeah, right. Newsflash: water is wet!" Other times, better other times, I was answered with an analogy to kudzu. (Didn't think I'd get there, did you?) "Sure, it's there, we all know it's there, but it's just not worth paying that much attention to, not worth noticing. What's the point anymore?" Except I think there is a point, maybe *the* point.

I'm still fascinated by the stuff, after all these years spent in the South. I've spent time arguing that there ought to be a traveling exhibition of kudzu sculpture, have philosophized about the stuff in academic literary circles: There's something about it, the way it "untells" a story, deconstructs it, blurs underlying definition, mystifying the original into something new and different and wonderful. . . . There was some lesson there that I just couldn't figure out, until recently. Other writers, southern writers especially, and maybe predictably, didn't really want to talk about it, didn't need to explain it, didn't need it explained, and frankly, were more than a little annoyed by the topic. It took a songwriter, a southern songwriter admittedly, Grayson Capps, to make some sense of it for me. He said that because life in the South was so clearly and inviolably demarcated—for most of its history, anyway—between acceptable and unacceptable, the privileged and oppressed, inside and outside, that storytelling developed a coding system—most obviously in blues music—to get your message out there, convey meaning, even share "inside" humor, express your "self" (which was so otherwise proscribed and stereotypical), air your grievances, or simply make a statement, a coding that continues and morphed into a "style," if you will, as a means of conveying levels of meaning, layers of significance. And then I remembered a quote I heard from Harry Belafonte. He said on NPR once, "The only way that we could speak to the pain and the anguish of our experiences was often through how we codified our stories in the songs that we sang." And I remembered thinking at the time, "What in the world must that feel like?" Taken together, then, it explains both my fascination with kudzu, and the inescapable sense of fraudulence whenever I'm lumped together, however haphazardly or arbitrarily, with what I consider authentic southern writers—one of whom I happen to live with, so it's an altogether familiar feeling.

But that's a good thing, I think, that feeling, of suspecting the notion that I'm ever going to put any "black on white" that is worthy of the ink spent is audacious, at best, more likely preposterous. I also suspect, moreover, it accounts for that common temptation to explain or excuse or justify the effort in the first place. And that can be a good thing, too. If the initial presumptive stance is that any word or words you propose to imbue with anything like permanence is unworthy, wouldn't that necessarily lend itself to the search for at least other words, maybe, even, with enough flagellation, better words? Too harsh, or hard? Not sure I've ever heard any writer—and if I did, it was met with absolute skepticism—claim it was easy. Every word should have that kind of value on it (as, say, back in Orwell's and Styron's and Hersey's and Irving's day, when writers were paid by the word), shouldn't it? But if you think that's too daunting, consider kudzu.

They say the Japanese perennial can grow up to a foot a day, can swallow whole buildings in a couple of months, smother thousands and thousands of acres a year, choking off any and all other native flora in the process. It's not unreasonable—setting aside whether it's metaphorically responsible—to suggest that we should all be so industrious, is it? And if that's not enough, if you feel cheated, for any reason, or just to end on a more positive note, then here, here's a recipe for kudzu blossom jelly:

- Wash kudzu blossoms with cold water, drain well and place them in a large bowl.
- Pour 4 cups boiling water over blossoms, and refrigerate 8 hours or overnight.
- Strain liquid through a colander into a Dutch oven, discarding blossoms.
- Add lemon juice and pectin; bring to a full rolling boil over high heat, stirring constantly.
- Stir in sugar; return to a full rolling boil, and boil, stirring constantly, 1 minute.
- Remove from heat; skim off foam with a spoon.
- Quickly pour jelly into hot, sterilized jars; filling to 1/4 inch from top.
- Wipe jar rims.
- Cover at once with metal lids, and screw on bands.
- Process in boiling water bath 5 minutes.
- Cool jars on wire racks.

Word is, it tastes a whole lot like grape jelly, which further validates—as if we need one—the monumental genius of George Washington Carver, right? But that's another story. . . .

The Meek Shall Inherit the Memoir: Then and Now

Harrison Scott Key

Some words I just don't like. They make me angry. Maybe it's the way these words feel in my mouth. Words like *chipotle* and *creamy* and *isthmus,* for example, have been known to make me violent. Show me a man who's going around talking about isthmuses, and I'll show you a man who's got problems. And can you imagine *creamy isthmuses?* Sounds like something they'd make you eat in Scandinavia. No thanks, Vikings!

Words are powerful things. You must know that, right? You're holding a whole magazine full of them. This magazine is basically an explosive device, when you think about it.

Ready to blow.

Speaking of *blow,* there's one word here that really blows.

Memoir.

It's French, for starters. A whole language invented to humiliate American patriots. The last time I said the word *œuvre* in public, people thought I was choking. I like a good solid consonant somewhere in my word, something I can build a house on. I need a *T.* If a *T* is not available, I'd like a *P* or a *B* or a *G.* A real *G,* not one of those *G*s that sounds like you're slowly drowning in a large bowl of *soupe à l'oignon.*

Memoir. How do you even say it?

Mem-*war?* Try it. You sound like a hillbilly.

Mem-**wah?** Now you sound like Ira Glass. Stop it.

Unfortunately, I spent much of my adult life trying to write the sort of thing described by this word I don't like.

"What are you working on?" friends would ask.

"Stories," I'd say.

"Short stories—cool!" they'd say.

"They're short, yes, but—"

"Not short stories?"

"They're stories, and they're short, but they're true."

"Oh. Like essays?"

"Sort of. About my family."

"So, it's like a memoir?"

I'd shudder.

It wasn't just the sound. It was the smell of the word. It smelled like self-importance. Like wretchedness and child abuse and alcoholism and sexual misdeeds. I started writing in the 1990s, the Decade of the Memoir, or rather the Decade of the Commonplace Autobiographies of Relatively Unimportant People and Celebrities Who Believed Their Stories Were Important. During the Clinton administration—maybe it was all the identity politics, the cancer of postcolonialism, who knows?—anybody who could get subjects and verbs to agree was trying to write a memoir that elevated his or her small lot of suffering into a Book of Job for the new millennium. Suddenly, people were writing books about overcoming ingrown toenails and having small nostrils. David Hasselhoff alone published, like, six memoirs from 1993–1997. These memoirs were more like long promotional brochures than books, but people bought them. Which was why they displayed them so prominently in bookstores, right out in front, near the books on how to become rich without the burden of intelligence or talent.

I wanted no part of this genre.

Genre.

Another French word.

Get away from me, French words! Go shave your legs or something!

Occasionally, I might find someone talking about a "great" or "genius" or "gripping" memoir, but I wrote it off to mass hysteria and instead turned my attention to the sort of thing I was trying to write back then, which was plays.

Play. That's a good word. It's fun, festive, familiar. Plays are raw, funny, deep. David Mamet, Tom Stoppard, Marsha Norman—geniuses.

"What are you writing?" friends would ask.

"A play."

"Awesome."

It was so easy!

Sometimes I found myself writing monologues, mostly for invented characters but sometimes with myself as the character, telling stories about people in my family. I'd been telling these stories for many years, mostly because these people, my family, were, to me, the most interesting people in the world, because they were insane.

A couple of years after 9/11, I stopped writing plays. I had many reasons for quitting, most of which had nothing to do with global jihad. Mostly, I was just bad at it.

The day after I quit writing plays, I went to a café with a notebook. I had decided I would write something new. I sat there, staring at the notebook, for about five years. This time, I blamed the secular humanists.

Then, five years later, in a moment of desperation, I went back to some of those funny monologues I'd written a long time before, and I erased all the stage directions and double-spaced everything, and the most amazing thing happened: the "dramatic monologues" shape-shifted into stories.

I went nuts. I started writing more and more of these stories, most of which were pretty bad, but not so bad that I wanted to cry.

"What are you working on?" friends asked during this happy new century.

"Stories," I said.

"Short stories, cool!" they said.

And I had to explain that these were not really made-up stories.

"So, it's like a memoir?"

"No, no, these are . . . essays."

Essays!

The word *essay* had a literary ring to it, a rich and aged patina and the scent of something serious, like a pair of old and well-polished boots—even if those boots were French, the word being so obviously Gallic in derivation, more vowel than consonant. But still, it was familiar and, more important, pronounceable. An essay could be a treatise, a philosophical declaration, a narrative postulation. Novelists, theologians, physicists, historians—they write essays. But to the average human being, even the kind who buys and reads books for fun and edification, reading essays probably sounds about as interesting as getting head lice—the only difference being, most people know where to get head lice. Good luck finding essays at your local bookstore. You're better off searching in the bookstore for the corpse of David Hasselhoff, who's probably not even dead yet, which would make his corpse pretty hard to find.

So I told people I was writing essays, and their eyes glazed over, and I dreamt of being a novelist or a better playwright so I could write things that people understood or, at least, things that would stave off the glazing of their eyes.

But I couldn't get away from my stories, which were, let's be honest, a lot like memoir. So I decided I should learn about the form. I mean, I was writing it; it only seemed honest to have read some. So I put on a gas mask and tied one end of a length of thread around the front door of a bookstore and the other end around my waist, and I went looking for the "memoir/autobiography/cry for help" shelf. When I found it, hidden out of embarrassment between "pets" and "fortune-telling," I saw the usual suspects: the celebrity and addiction and abuse memoirs. I found one by Tori Spelling and opened to a random page, just to see what sort of wonders it might unleash upon my mind. It couldn't be *that* bad. *Somebody* had published it. The passage I came to said this: "I have a pretty detailed short-term memory. I can read a script once and remember all my lines—for the next day at least."

Just reading that made my brain hurt. It didn't matter if it was true. Actually, it did. If it was true, then I think people would pay to see it. You could lock up Ms. Spelling in a vault and give her a script—let's say for something really good, like *Hedda Gabler*—and there'd be a camera in the vault so viewers at home could watch her read the script once, and then she'd be let out of the vault and forced to perform in a live production of the play, and if she didn't remember all her lines, they'd throw her back in the vault, except this time with a Kodiak bear.

There were a lot of books like Tori Spelling's. Books by people who'd overcome cancer, AIDS, blackness, whiteness, wealth, insanity, and asymmetrical thumbs. Yet, moving these volumes aside with a pair of tongs, I found other books whose first pages read remarkably like novels, like this strange one by Nabokov: "The cradle rocks above an abyss, and common sense tells us that our existence is but a brief crack of light between two eternities of darkness."

It was so, so, so *bleak*. I loved it!

The celebrity/heroin/polio memoirs were all strangely upbeat throughout, as if to reassure readers that even a story about giving birth to cloven-hoofed twins in an opium den can have a happy ending. But these other memoirs— they were fantastically honest about the banal terrors and fleeting joys of quotidian existence. Like . . . like . . . like *literature*.

I read them all and came to the conclusion that writing memoir did not automatically make one a jackass. I practiced saying it in the mirror.

"Memoir," I said to myself. "**Mem**-war. **Mem**-war. **Mem**-war." It sounded like *memory war*, which was maybe more accurate than I knew.

At first, saying it was hard. I sort of retched a little, the way children do when you make them eat French food, such as the pancreas of small cattle. But I got better. I tried different phrasings: Memoir. Memoir essays. Autobiographical stories.

The only other problem I had, the one that wouldn't go away, was my belief that people who wrote memoirs were pathological narcissists.

I mean, who did I think I was? Who would want to read about me? The only real answer I could come up with: my mother. The other answer: this is a dumb question. Because everybody's boring, and everybody's interesting, and some mothers are heartless, and some can't even read.

The better question: how do I map the expressionist strangeness of my inner life in a way that invites others to sit in the cockpit of my soul and soar through the atmosphere of me, which is the only me I've ever been and the only unique thing I possess anyway?

And the answer: I don't know. It's hard.

And the other answer: get over it.

And: God loves you even if nobody else does.

And: make yourself the bad guy. (See: *Black Boy*)

And: make it about other people. (See: *The Boys of My Youth*)

And: make it a love letter to people you love. (See: *Speak, Memory*)

And: make it about alien things. (See: *Out of Africa*)

And: make it beautiful. (See: *Wind, Sand, and Stars*)

And: be humble. (See: Ecclesiastes)

Seriously, be humble.

Which means you might have to humiliate yourself.

Don't lie about your fake superhuman ability to memorize scripts.

Unless you're willing to prove it on television.

With bears.

These days, if you ask me about my new book, I'll tell you.

"It's a memoir," I'll say. And if you ask me what it's about, I'll tell you the truth: it's about how I overcame my fear of creamy isthmuses.

Which is at least as true as Tori Spelling's memoir.

The Ghost of Josiah King

Cassandra King

After all these years, I'm finally out of the closet. I can call myself a writer. Not only that, I write for a living, and sort of support myself doing so. I got off to a late start, but I've finally gotten to the place I've been heading all my life. Even though I didn't spend nearly enough time earlier in my career worrying about when or how, *why* was always clear to me. I'm a writer because of my gene pool.

Let me explain. Writing is really the only thing I've ever wanted to do. With the exception of my horse years as a kid, when my love of riding made me long to be a cowgirl (or secretly, a cowboy), I never had any other ambition. Growing up in the fifties, my girlfriends wanted to be nurses or teachers, either before marrying and raising a family, or after the kids started school and they had free time on their hands. Not me. As a child, I was different from my playmates. I lived in my own little world, a world of make-believe. At the missionary society, my mother bragged to the church ladies that I was no trouble at all. I was a quiet little thing, who was good about entertaining myself and my little sisters. That is, when I didn't have my nose stuck in a book, my mother would add. Stories, she said with a laugh. That girl loved her a good story.

She got that right, and I was lucky to come from a family of great storytellers. My grandfather could always be persuaded to tell tales of the good old days, when he was a boy and survived hard times. But the best stories came from my father and his brother, my Uncle Rex. Both of them could tell ghost stories that scared the holy hell out of my sisters and me. We were terrified of the Wampus Kitty living in the swamp near our house, whose cry was like the scream of a woman. Both Daddy and Uncle Rex swore they had heard her/it. And both of them told us about the time they had been chased by Old Bloody Bones, one dark night when they were walking home from Aunt Fenny-Rump's. Aunt Fenny-Rump was an African American medicine woman who lived in a cabin in the woods, and they'd been sent to fetch one of her remedies. She warned the boys about Old Bloody Bones, a haunt who was wrapped in bloody rags and had a voracious appetite for children, but they didn't believe her until he came after them.

Once I learned to write, I made up my own stories and put them to paper. I started out by recording tales of the Wampus Kitty, Old Bloody Bones, and Aunt Fenny-Rump, who scared me almost as much as the other two. (Surely she was a *witch!*) Then I expanded my répertoire, making up fairy tales, ghost stories, and other adventures. Some of my stories became plays, which I staged with my dolls and stuffed animals, my little sisters serving as a captive audience. I took my stories to school to read to my classmates. They loved the ghost stories most of all and begged for more. That turned into my first paying gig. When I read ghost stories aloud during recess, I learned to stop at a crucial point, just before the bell rang. To hear the next chapter, you had to share your snack. I racked up with Hershey bars, apples or oranges, little boxes of raisins. It became my first lesson in writing: to keep my readers' interest, I had to leave them wanting more.

Even though I was a successful, paid author at an early age, eventually I was forced to go underground. My career path was breaking my mother's heart. I had been such a good little girl, and now this! Flush with success, I couldn't wait to share my stories with the family, imagining how proud they'd be. One night after supper, before the dishes were done and my sisters and I excused from the table, I asked everyone to stay put so I could read to them. They obliged, probably assuming my performance was part of an assignment. But when I read a story and proudly proclaimed myself the author, only my sisters applauded. Instead of the pride I expected, my father regarded me with dismay. My mother shook her head sadly, then reported my shenanigans the very next day. Soon the extended family chimed in. My grandparents tsk-tsked, and my beloved aunts and uncles demanded that my parents straighten me out before it was too late. I had shown my true colors and proven to everyone that, alas, I had inherited the genes of the only other writer in the family—my great-grandfather, Josiah King.

You'd think having a relative who was a published writer would be a source of pride for the family, but no. As far as I know, I'm the only one who has ever shown any appreciation. Although I didn't know Grandpa King very well, I knew from an early age that he was a writer with two books to his credit. I don't remember exactly when I first saw his books, but I must've been pretty young. I recall the moment clearly, when I held his small brown book of Alabama history in my hands and stared at it in awe. Since I revered books, it blew my mind that a relative of mine had written one. His other publication was more of a chapbook, a little delicately bound book of poetry. I poured over both of them wide-eyed. Now, I realize that the poems were god-awful, but at my tender age, I thought they were better than Edgar Allan Poe's, whose style Grandpa King copied. If Poe had still been around, there might've been a lawsuit. The poems were long, overwrought elegies to his long-dead wife, a great-grandmother I never knew, and I remember lines like "Methought I saw my dear dead Amanda appearing as in a dream!"

The King family's disdain of my great-grandfather's accomplishment wasn't because they were illiterate philistines with no appreciation of learning. Although my father, the oldest son who came of age during the depression, didn't have the opportunity for a college education, his brothers and sisters did. Uncle Rex was a Bama graduate, and even my grandmother and a great-aunt had gone to college, very unusual for women of their day. Plus, they were a family of avid readers. I was taught at a young age that books were expensive possessions to be treasured. Our family gatherings involved discussions of what one was currently reading. My mother and aunts swapped their Book-of-the-Month Club selections with each other, my father and uncles their war sagas and westerns. I loved spending time at my grandparents' house because I had unlimited access to their bookcases and a secluded window seat where I curled up to read.

No, it was something else. Had Josiah King been a commercial success as a writer, I have no doubt that attitudes would have been different. Instead, he was considered a fool and a dreamer. The family, hard workers who were mostly farmers, felt that Grandpa King wasted his time writing when he could be doing something—anything!—more productive. No one is quite sure what Josiah King did for a living. A "gentleman farmer," he was a ne'er-do-well who wrote a weekly column for the county newspaper (for very little pay) between halfheartedly farming his crops. My father explained it this way: Grandpa King married well, or the family would have been poverty-stricken. Evidently my great-grandmother, Amanda Clark, did what most of us southern women do, and married beneath her.

Since Grandpa King was an old man when I was born, I didn't know him well. I remember him as being grumpy and imposing, far from the cuddly, grandfatherly type. A large man, bald as a coot, he cut an impressive figure, walking around town with the aid of a dapper silver-domed cane. In my memories he's sort of a dandy, dressed in white linen suits, with a gold watch fob. Always chewing on a cigar and wearing a hat, he looked like Sir Winston in his latter days. Grandpa King was a regular at First Methodist, and would embarrass me when he rapped his cane on the floor and cried "Amen!" during the sermon.

I was thirteen when he died in my grandfather's house, at age ninety. As was the custom in those days, my grandparents had taken him in after he grew infirm and unable to live alone. When I visited, I was often called upon to take him a tray. I'll always regret that I never got up the nerve to talk to him about writing. Not only was I painfully shy at that age, I was ill at ease with him. I had plenty of opportunity to chat: his bedroom was filled with the books he'd brought with him, and he asked me once if I liked to read. When I nodded, he told me to help myself to any of his books. What a missed opportunity! If only I'd asked about the books he wrote, or his columns, or if he'd always been a writer. I imagine he was sick and lonely and would've welcomed company and conversation. But I blew it. Instead I grabbed a book off the shelf and scurried out to the window seat, anxious to get away from his intimidating presence.

Josiah King died shortly afterwards, but he never really left. Even my most skeptical relatives admit that his ghost haunts the house, even to this day. There are just too many unexplained noises and sightings for anyone to deny. When my grandmother died a few years later, my family moved into my grandparents' home while our new house was being built. Late at night my little sisters would run to my room and crawl in bed with me when we heard the clump-clump-clump of a cane coming up the stairs. Sometimes an unseen presence played the piano downstairs. My mother was impatient with our fears and insisted it was the cat. (The only piano-playing cat in Alabama!) But our daddy got it. He told us to hush up and go to sleep. It was just Grandpa King, and we knew good and well that he wouldn't bother us.

My sisters didn't care who it was; they didn't want any spirits hanging around playing the piano and clomping up the stairs. But I liked knowing that it was Grandpa King. His ghost haunts me to this day. Poor old fellow. I wonder what it must have been like for him to be considered a dreamer and a fool because he had rather write books and poems than plow a field? He must have felt like a failure, even with his two books to show for his efforts. No one in the family remembers the title of either book or who published them. Could he have published them himself, I asked my father a few years ago? Daddy laughed and shook his head. No way he could've afforded to, he said, and neither could Grandma King, although she had been quite well-to-do until her unfortunate marriage. My father had no idea what had happened to the books I remembered seeing, which breaks my heart. I hate to think this, but I figure the books were thrown away after Grandpa King died, tossed out as useless, not even worth donating to charity.

So I write for all the usual reasons—can't do anything but; have an overactive imagination; was raised in the South around great storytellers; have always loved books and reading; and am happier when writing than anything else in the world. But there's another reason that's become pretty obvious to me. Writing is in my blood. Somehow, of all the descendants of Josiah King, I was the one to inherit the genetic disposition, a great-granddaughter that he barely knew. I'm certainly a dreamer, and admit to being a bit of a fool. No other occupation but writing holds any interest for me. Grandpa King, it seems that a part of you is still alive in me.

I have no trouble believing that the ghost of Josiah King still walks the halls of the old home place. He's probably looking for his long-lost books. If the house were still in the family, I'd love to camp out there one night and help him look. Although there's little chance of finding his books, maybe I could leave him with one of mine. I like to think he'd be pleased that his love of writing was passed on to a great-granddaughter who is proud to share his bloodline.

The Agoraphobic Writer

Corey Mesler

Writing is all about getting to do more. It would be very boring for
me to have to live my life over again, I just want to live somebody
else's. I hate to travel, but writing a novel is like taking a long trip.
This way I can stay peacefully at home.

—ANNE TYLER

*W*riting is a lonely, solitary life. Unlike one who makes movies,
or plays in a band, or plays soccer, a writer sits alone in his
or her study with the tools that can take an aggregation of
twenty-six letters and ten numbers and make them dance in some inspired
way, whether pinned to a sheet of foolscap, or made of fairy dust like the new
digitalized media. The writer doesn't, very often, get group help with the work
at hand: which gerund is worthiest, or whether to use the Oxford comma,
or which voice sounds best, first person, second, or third. Often the writer
might think that no voice is best. I have had days when I thought no voice
is best. Silence is golden. It is also giving up. Normally—whether the writer
is a poet or fictionist or memoirist—he or she sits and tries to pull from the
ether a coherent *something*: a freak, an incubus, a chirpy infant.

So, in short, a writer spends a lot of time alone indoors. If there are parties
sometimes the writer goes. If there are other writer friends sometimes there
are get-togethers, commiseration, shrugs, guarded iteration of current work,
even shared joy. But, these parties or indeed any outside stuff, including read-
ings and signings, book promotion, etc., make up a small percentage of the
life the writer has chosen. It's mostly the other thing, the rainy-day solitaire.

Now: I am often told that I am a prolific writer. What this means is that I am frequently a year away from the publication of a new book, and that I am *always* enmeshed in the intricate calisthenics of writing a new one. I have published a bit, a number of novels, a handful of collections of poems or short stories, and I feel lucky about this because I started late. I did not publish my first novel until I was 40 years old. If this makes me blue I remind myself that W. C. Fields made his best movie, *The Bank Dick,* when he was 60.

However, here is the not-so-secret secret to my late but fertile success: I have agoraphobia. What this means is that I don't leave my home easily. What this means is that I leave my house rarely. What this means is that I have a lot of free time on my hands, and, I mean, crikey, I gotta do something with it. Chained to my desk, each cockcrow, I write, even on tough mornings, even when the cacodemon of anxiety sits on my chest sucking the air from my lungs and the ink from my imaginary biro, even when I am grieving for my country, even when I am too cold, or too hot, or too tired, or too nauseated, or too lazy. It's a spur to creativity, this *lusus naturae* malady, though, friends, I don't recommend agoraphobia as a healthy spur to creativity. The hours are good but the cost to the soul is deadly. If not for my wife and children I would probably have a soul that croaked too early like Buddy Holly, a soul that looks like that bit of overdone chicken fat at the bottom of the broiler.

Illnesses can be thought of as teachers (in our more optimistic moments) and agoraphobia is a teacher with a cat-o'-nine tails. I listened because I had to. Mind over matter is all well and good, but if matter makes you shake and shimmy and your bowels boogie, for the most part, matter's got a better hand than mind does. I was in therapy for over a dozen years, most of that time with a Jungian Zen dream analyst, and, though it deepened me, made me a better writer, made me even perhaps a better person, it did not make leaving my home easier. I formulated a bargain with myself: I will live with this and I will attempt to act as if it doesn't affect the me that really matters, the me with, you know, a poetic *soul.* Soul is, perhaps, too easy a word (I looked in vain for a better synonym), too much a buzzword like the guy at the party who does sleight-of-hand to get attention. But, then, I have lived almost my entire life (so far) in Memphis, Tennessee, a place on maps, real and illusory, known for its soul, in every permutation of the term. Memphis is in me as much as I am in Memphis.

About the teacher thing: One of the first things agoraphobia taught me was that I was going to be alone a lot. Eventually friends stopped inviting me to do things. Eventually some friends fell away. And I am often left feeling as if everyone else is out participating in the great human ridotto while I am isolated at home, working on poems, working on a new novel, watching Turner Classic Movies, or daydreaming about Jessica Chastain. It can be thought of as a comfortable prison cell because it's home, but it's still a prison cell. All my familiars are around me: my books, my keyboard, my Beatles and Dylan, my DVDs, my potpies, my drum set, my Matchbox cars, my collection of *Cracked* magazine; so, it's even a seductive prison cell. And it's all okay, this bear trap on my ankle, except the days it's not. After missing my daughter's one violin concert I could only feel shame, burning shame and self-loathing, ditto any of the many family get-togethers out of state. And I am often jealous hearing about friends' trips to the beach, to Florence, to San Francisco, to Truth or Consequences, New Mexico, to the Lesser Hebrides. I never thought I wanted to see the Lesser Hebrides until I found out I couldn't.

Now, listen: some days, even if I'm authoring away, I feel like a waste of harvestable organs. I stare into the middle distance and the middle distance pulls down its blinds. Some days I am Philboyd Studge, to use Vonnegut's name for the oaf inside who inhibits good writing. But some days—O days of fire!—I feel like I could outbox Papa. Those days are writing's gift. Without writing God knows where I'd be, cut off from humanity on a little island of self-pity with no Turner Classic Movies or Memphis Grizzlies games to save me. I would be Robinson Curse-oh.

My wife says that agoraphobia fits our lifestyle. This is true: neither of us is very social and wouldn't be throwing many merrymakings even if I were not so afflicted. But it's similar to that crafty feature of the Garden of Eden: being told not to eat of the Tree of Knowledge only makes one want to eat of the Tree of Knowledge. Sometimes, I want that fruit so badly I drown in defeatism and misery. It reminds me of one of my favorite lines from the movie *The Holly and the Ivy*: "I suppose those people who fall asleep in the snow feel like this. They know they've got to keep awake at all costs; but they can't help giving up the struggle just for a moment, because the snow's so warm and cosy." So, giving up is not an option, right? Because as humans, gifted with the variegated world, we are expected to soldier on. Beckett: *I can't go on. I'll go on.*

And I do not mean to say that "the agoraphobic writer" is any more interesting than anyone else. As a friend says, everyone has something, and this probably goes double for creative folk. I do not mean that agoraphobia is interesting, or funny, or grist for the mill. Mental health problems are terrible and more so because they are invisible. Anyone looking at me might see only an old fart with a sardonic grin. Underneath the surface flows the dark, chthonic Styx.

But, back to writing. Just being prolific is not the only benefit of having all this isolated time on my hands. In a very real sense my writing goes out into the world for me. To get a poem published in *Poetry*, as I did in 2015, is like getting an invitation to follow the yellow brick road. To publish a new novel and have a friend see it in a bookstore in faraway Rockaway is balm. I am being read in Peoria! Sometimes I even get a fan email. This is the big stamp of approval; this is the golden ticket to the chocolate factory.

Writing is a very real lifeline for me. I am standing on the island and I am saved by a line I throw out myself. It might be grandiose to say that writing saved my life—certainly it did not in the dramatic fashion of poor Janet Frame, who was about to be lobotomized before her work was discovered—but without my little literary envois my life would be a diminished thing.

So, go, little poem, I say. I cast you upon the waters like bread; make love to the world for me (to scramble and strangle my metaphors). Little lyric scribble: Tell everyone that I am fine and doing well, locked, as I am, in the castle's turret. I have my fellow authors encased in cloth and glue all around me like a fairy ring. I have my word machine, my imagination, my cup of tea. I have my dreams, a picture of Yeats above me, my steely eye, my sweet and sour memories, and a really good thesaurus.

And, to close, as the after-dinner speakers say, I offer this from Robert Bly: "The fundamental world of poetry is an inward world. We approach it through solitude." I live in the fundamental world.

II

Becoming a *Southern* Writer

I have always tried to write of this South in a way beyond clichés, and that is why, most often, I have pulled my writings from the memories and stories of my own blood. The most interesting thing about my South is not juleps on the veranda and sweet tea in a Mason jar (though I have enjoyed both). There is more to us than deer hunting, or NASCAR; the Yankees have all but wrestled that from us, anyway. There is more to us, even, than football, and no matter how many sportscasters might say it, it is not truly our religion; it engenders far too much cursing for that, though we have prayed to our Lord and Savior on third down and three, and like to tell that joke about St. Peter walking on water in Bear Bryant's hat.

—RICK BRAGG, *MY SOUTHERN JOURNEY*

What Happens Next

Patti Callahan Henry

When I was nine years old, I lied to my parents. I'm sure I'd lied before and I know I did so again, but *this* time sent me to the page to pen my first story.

At our summer cottage in Cape Cod, Massachusetts, my sister and I were on the lake in our tiny Sailfish sailboat. My dad (the pastor) and mom were sitting on the shore's edge with their friends. They reclined on multicolored blankets and folding metal beach chairs, all serene. It was, if such a thing is possible, a picturesque day. These were the long lazy days of summer when time stretched and all the world seemed to be waiting patiently on the other side of August. But then my sister Barbi did something or said something that is lost to the annals of time. Whatever it was, I didn't like it and I called her a bad name, a name that began with a b.

I don't have a quiet voice; I never have. So that b name rolled across the calm blue waters and landed on the shoreline where my parents sat. When my sister and I returned with the sailboat, we crawled out of that little vessel, and in front of everyone, my dad confronted me. I lied. "No, I did not use that bad name. I called her a brat."

No one believed me, but the day went on in peace. But as a good little girl who then believed in hell and damnation, that untruth haunted me. At that age, I couldn't process why I hadn't told the truth about such a minor infraction, one that would have brought down "discipline" but not so bad in the long run. So I typed up a story on my dad's typewriter, the old Remington that sat on the kitchen table, which he used to write his sermons. It was a story about a girl who told one little lie and then watched her world unravel.

I drew a cover, colored it, and stapled it together. My mom read the story and then smiled at me. "Is there something you want to tell me?"

I confessed.

I write for as many reasons as there are stories, but it was this initial impetus—to find out what might happen after a lie—that has been the seed from which my stories have grown.

I believe I've been doing the same thing ever since—taking my questions, my hopelessness, my wonderings, and even my fascination with the world, to the page. It is there that I have the power to make a choice, to change an outcome, to project forward to what *might* happen next.

There are other reasons, too, of course. I write because I don't know many other ways to process the world around me. I write because, since childhood, story has been both my sustenance and also my support. I write because I don't know what I believe or understand until I write it down. I write because there's nothing else I do as well or as frequently or with as much desire. I write because the stories inside have to go somewhere, so why not on paper? I write because I'm addicted to the rare moment when it finally works and comes together like magic. I write to bypass despair.

I'm not sure anyone can untangle all of the motives for choosing to do what we do with our days and with our hours. I'm sure there are subconscious reasons whispering and influencing all my choices, childhood being the greatest compost pile of them all.

When I was twelve years old, my dad's job caused a family move from a quiet enclave in the Northeast to south Florida. Culture shock is an understatement. From a brick sidewalk stroll to the junior high under oak and willow trees to a concrete world ensconced in enough humidity to drown me. To sit in my heart during that time would have been to feel a confused, scared, and lonely girl who didn't know why she must begin again in such a strange world. It was during this time that I found the sanctuary of libraries and of stories. I started a lifelong habit of reading not for escape but to understand the world, to *somehow* comprehend how it worked and why what happens next does, because nothing made sense to me.

So why would the reasons for writing be any different than the reasons for reading? I aspire to unravel the reasons and the motivations behind actions, which can never be fully understood but can be approached gently and carefully with just the right language. We must "be present" in each moment for positive mental health, but sometimes it is necessary to look forward, to know there is another corner, and around that corner something else will happen. Nothings stays the same.

We all wrestle with the unknown, but I believe writers have a hidden limp from all that wrestling.

I create a world and then toss into that world a conundrum. Then I watch as I try to write my way out of it. I can ask: If I set this character up for a fall, what will they do? What will occur to save or harm them? I ask a question and then take it to the far extreme, watch it unfold into the future.

Embedded within the inquiry, "What happens next?" I believe there exists a hidden seed of hope, because no matter where we are (or where our character is), or how bad it is, something always happens next. This isn't merely a question to spur the writing forward, but to enliven our days, to allow hope to infuse some of the darker times.

During my childhood I was often chastised for what now serves me— living in two worlds. "Get your head out of the clouds" was a line I heard more times than I can count. I still live in that dual world—the one where I am alive and present with my life, with my family, with my loved ones, but also (there is no duplicity here) with my stories. It can be disorienting, yes, but also satisfying, because sometimes these vivid worlds overlap and the writing informs the living and the living informs the writing.

I'm often labeled a "southern writer," and this makes me preen because these are my favorite kinds of authors. But what does this mean for a writer who was born in New Jersey and grew up in Philadelphia?

Although the bulk of my adolescence was spent in south Florida, I didn't understand what "southern" meant until I attended Auburn University in Alabama. It was there that the external geography began to form my internal landscape, alter the shape of my soul.

My first view of Alabama was of a mysterious, lush land that oddly felt more like home than anywhere had in years. Home, I realized, could be chosen.

It took me a long while to adjust to this new milieu where the Civil War was still being talked about as if it happened the year before, where the fraternities on campus celebrated "Old South" as girls donned antebellum dresses to ride in parades in pickup trucks (I was one of them; my dress was pink), where football was a religion with rites of passage and stern reverence. It was all so new to me—so much nostalgia for days gone by. What was this?

The lyrical, lovely accents lured me in, and I emulated them in an attempt both meager and also embarrassing. My northern history was obdurate; I couldn't fabricate a new past, but I could find my way into a heritage I was coming to admire.

I'm sure my view of the South is vastly different from those who grew up in its lush storytelling cradle. But sometimes an outside eye has more appreciation for what might otherwise be taken for granted. When I write about the landscape, I bring to each sentence a kind of reverence for the place I didn't truly discover until adulthood.

Then I found Pat Conroy. Then I found Anne Rivers Siddons, and I began to understand what the South could and did mean *for* me. As Faulkner said, "The past is never dead." In the stories and friendships, I sensed a melancholy, not that I could have named it as such in those days, permeated the history of families and individuals. Ritual and ceremonial tradition, which I'd once only seen in the church, were part of family and societal life in a way I hadn't experienced before. For me, the South became a land of wistful stories, a place where what happened before mattered as much as what happened now—it was all tangled together to make us who we are. I don't know if this is what the South means to a born and bred in the wool southerner, but it is what it means to me.

I sensed that each time a story was told, it altered slightly, changing its shape and meaning with each retelling. I finally decided that if I could shape a life by reading and writing stories, what higher calling could I have? (Many I'm sure, but that's how it felt to me.)

So I write about the South, southern families, southern landscape, and the pensive loss of the past that seems to permeate the area. My stories, all of them so far, are set in the South, and in a very particular area: the coast from North Carolina to Alabama. My novels are the means I've used to insert myself into a world from whence I didn't begin, a place steeped in history of which I have no part.

It is often said that setting is a character, and I think that's true, but for me southern setting is the metaphor, it is the petri dish from which my stories grow and become what they are meant to be.

I didn't begin in the South, but I sure have stayed here, always looking and keeping my eye out for what might happen next.

Stardust:
An Essay on Voice in Four Parts

Sonja Livingston

To me, the greatest pleasure of writing is not what it's about,
but the inner music that words make.
—TRUMAN CAPOTE

I.

*I*n the summer of 1977, my sister Stephanie took to saying *fixing to*, which, in our neighborhood, was abbreviated to *finna*. Steph was a tomboy who hung out with the toughest kid on the street and she and Junior were always fixing to do something. They were *finna build a fort, finna go to the corner store for a pack of Bubble Yum, finna climb three flights of stairs to launch plastic soldiers from the roof.*

I watched from a distance, burning with envy. I wasn't jealous of Junior or the plastic soldiers, but of my sister. She went wherever she wanted and refused to comb her mane of black hair, no matter how often my mother told her it looked like a rat's nest. Now she was breaking the rules again. We were white girls in a northern city; saying *finna* was just not done. Except, here was Stephanie, declaring what she was *finna do* fifty times a day.

It's not as if we were proper. We all wore cheap sneakers and hand-me-downs from older siblings in that neighborhood. All of us had single mothers, absentee fathers, and qualified for free lunch at school. We were Puerto Rican. We were African American. We were white. Mostly this did not matter. When we roamed the streets of northeast Rochester or sat scrounging money for pizza on someone's front porch, no one noticed the shade of the hand from which the last quarter came. Other times, color was everything. It dictated the foods we ate. How we did our hair. The words we heard from our mothers so often, the sound of them was traced onto our cells.

The Puerto Rican girls said *mira* and *que linda* and *ay Dios mio.* Their words were a delicious stew of syllables, and when they occasionally descended into profanity, even their cursing sounded pretty. The black girls snapped their gum and said *all ya'll need to be quiet* and *my Aunt Jewel trying to sleep up in here,* making *aunt* rhyme with *taunt* and *flaunt.* Their voices rung out loud and clear from open windows, the rhyme of their *all y'alls* just about undid me. White girls said *pop* in place of *soda,* allowed the regional tightness of vowels to smother our various ethnic inheritances, but sounded otherwise like people on TV. I was not happy with my lot. I wanted to possess the timbre and beat of every word I'd ever heard, but except for my sister adopting *finna* that summer, most of us kept to our own sounds.

Still, I tried. I went to the Rosas' house for dinner and learned to say *sí* when rice and beans were offered and *no, gracias* when it was pork. I watched the girls at school and wondered if I might ever learn to speak with such color and force. Mostly, I waited and watched and stuffed myself with sounds that got tripped up on my tongue—and, not just words, but their tones and spirals and upswings. So many words and sounds abound in even one city neighborhood, each with their own feel and sensibility and pull. I scooped them up and stored them like gold coins in the basket of my head.

II.

Twenty years later, I made it through high school and college and out of the neighborhood. After years of working and studying, I finally sat back and relaxed enough to remember all those words jangling around unspent, and considered how I might use them. I could speak them, of course, but even as an adult, I preferred to make most of my noise on the page. I joined a writing group, took a community workshop, and eventually signed up for a five-week writing workshop in Prague. Every night someone stood up on stage and read. We were in the Czech Republic, surrounded by statues and castles and gilded spires, but the program was sponsored by the University of New Orleans and we might as well have been in Baton Rouge for the sultry cluck of voices. For five weeks, I listened to Czech during the day and the sounds of the American South at night. Tuscaloosa. Bogalusa. Lafayette. Little Rock. My head was like a cookie dipped in coffee, everything saturating until things softened and loosened. I had to go all the way to Eastern Europe to hear the supple consonants and lush vowels of my own country. I still remember the look on the Alabaman's face as she rattled off a list of southern writers, none of whom I knew. Exasperated, she finally asked: *Have you heard of Flannery O' Connor, at least?*—which I realized was the equivalent of asking if I'd ever heard of Jesus Christ. *Yes,* I said, while she side-eyed me and remained unconvinced.

I ended up joining the graduate writing program, choosing the New Orleans program not so much for the course offerings or faculty but because I was hooked by what I'd heard.

What broke open that summer was my hunger for voice. I wanted to use my stash of words to experience the direct connection between gut and tongue, without the great sifting out of the head. In fact, for all the differences in culture, it wasn't how exotic the southern voice sounded that won me over, but how intimately familiar. What the southern writer set out like colorful laundry flapping on a line, I'd learned to keep folded and tucked away. Our various cultures may tell us what we can and cannot do with words, but the sounds are there, caught and buzzing, waiting to be set free. For the first time since I was a child, language was on fire in me. It wasn't only the southern voices that fueled the fire, but rural writers, Jewish writers, African American writers—anyone who'd ever been told they weren't worthy of being heard. People who had been made to feel ashamed of their dialects and sat on their local phrases, until their words became like gems buried under layers of muck, made harder and more brilliant by the years of pressing down, so that when the people finally spoke, diamonds fell from open mouths.

III.

Flash forward fifteen years. Springtime in Tennessee. I was invited to speak at a conference in Oak Ridge. *Perfect,* I thought when the invitation came, *I'll get to drive to the mountains, and talk about voice.* But when the day came, I was late to pick up a rental car and the only car left was a Fiat, whose controls were as foreign to me as its tiny size. I was about thirty miles outside of Memphis by the time I figured out how to roll up the windows. My contact lenses had dried from the wind rushing into the car. The sun was high and I'd forgotten my sunglasses. Add to that construction slowdowns and heavy traffic. If that weren't enough, I was beginning to question who I was and what on God's green earth I was thinking when I decided to attend a conference of southern writers to talk about voice—what could an introverted woman from Rochester, New York, possibly have to tell anyone from east Tennessee?

All of this—the dry eyes and blinding sun and me running frantic, until finally, I stopped. Somewhere near Nashville, I pulled into a Pilot station and grabbed a pair of leopard-frame sunglasses, a diet Dr. Pepper, and two CDs from the $5.99 music bin—Loretta Lynn singing hymns and Willie Nelson singing pop standards.

I unwrapped the Willie Nelson CD with my teeth and slipped it into the player. As soon as he started singing "Stardust," things began to let up. By the time he got to "Unchained Melody" I was crying for how sad and sweet the sound, but was wholly put back together again by "Don't Get Around Much Anymore." I sang along in the tiny car, beginning to notice the dogwoods and redbuds blooming along Highway 40. Everything was all right. Better than all right.

It's possible that the leopard-frame sunglasses and the cold soda assisted in my revival. Certainly the songs (their arrangements and time-worn lyrics) were moving, but what really turned things around enough to make me notice the earth in blossom was the sound of a single human voice.

What is it about one true and resonant voice? Why and how can it change the way I feel about myself and open my eyes to what's around me? Willie Nelson's voice was nothing short of transformative. It not only soothed me, but served as a channel between myself and the larger beauty outside me. The essayist Brian Doyle says that: *All stories are, in some form, prayers.* Which means that all writers are, in some form, praying, and what I'm suggesting is that perhaps it's not only the words we use but their shape and sound that matter. This makes sense when you consider that even before we developed our own voices, we were enfolded by the swish and pulse of our mother's bodies. Which means that, as writers, it's our job to not only watch, but to set our ear upon the surface of the world and take it all in.

IV.

Prior to the Renaissance, people believed that the human voice emanated from the heart. Science soon explained that this was not the case. While I understand that anatomically speaking, a voice can't come from the heart, poetically speaking, everything is possible, and it seems to me that our most important voices come not from the throat but through the heart.

Writers spend much time discussing voice. We like to talk about diction and syntax, style and persona. What we often forget, however, is that voice is acoustic. Pure sound. Rhythm, timbre, and pitch. An imprint so personal, it's how we find each other in the dark. So when we talk about finding our voices, I wonder how we can ever lose something closer to us than the flesh. In fact, I sometimes think the entire matter of writing can be boiled down to whether or not we connect with the voice on the page. So much is about forging a connection with the reader, and so much about connection boils down to not what we say, but how we say it. So while I talk with my students about craft and dialogue and sensory details—and believe me, I could lose my mind over a great detail—beneath it all, what we really crave is the sound of a human voice rising from the page, saying: *Listen. Here I am. We are together now.*

What makes a good voice depends on your preferences, I suppose, but I find the best voice is a true voice. One that doesn't try to impress or put on airs. One of the greatest mistakes new writers make is to try to sound writerly which ends up cheating them of the best thing they have going for them. Words like *finna* and *mira* and *all y'all.* Our personal caches of language. Stewing for years, overused at times, or overlooked entirely—they are our toolkits, the material we use to build bridges to others, and to the lost parts of ourselves.

Such a simple thing, the human voice. But no less miraculous for its simplicity. The fact that with twenty-six letters and a handful of punctuation marks, one human being can distill and transmit sound to another human being thousands of miles and hundreds of years away is astounding, isn't it? That I can pick up a poem or story and hear the sound of struggle or celebration is what keeps me coming back to books. Voice is the magic of writing. If character and setting form the body of a story, voice is the breath that transforms it into a living thing.

We tend to doubt our stories, our voices, what we have to contribute, and whether anyone will care. In a world of fast and easy entertainment, we wonder if we put our voices out there, will anyone even hear. *But what if no one even reads it?* My students sometimes ask. And while I understand insecurity and wanting to be heard, how the work is received is beside the point.

We have to remind ourselves of our riches. Of the importance of what we have within us—all that we've seen and heard and stored away. We have an obligation to our words, to the people who said them, and to what we know to be real in the world. Your particular stories and the beautiful sounds that only you can make is what will save us during troubled times. When we let ourselves sing—really sing—what comes from within us belongs not just to you or me, but to all of us. This never stops amazing me. One true voice. Nothing less than stardust.

How I Became a Southerner

Sally Palmer Thomason

I have this weird feeling I've landed in the wrong book. This is an anthology of southern writers and if you peruse my pedigree, you, most likely, will question if my credentials are bona fide. Psychologists tell us that the experiences and relationships in our early lives, our formative years, largely shape our sense of place and who we become. Flannery O'Connor, one of the South's most distinguished writers, when asked what one should write about, said, "Anybody who has survived his childhood has enough information about life to last him the rest of his days."

I was not born in the South. I did not spend my formative years in the South. I was born and raised almost two thousand miles from the geographic center of what is designated by the geographers and historians as "The South." My first steps, and later school matriculations and graduations, occurred in California, nearly one thousand miles from "The South's" westernmost border. My toes never touched a speck of southern soil until after I'd become an adult. What's more, to my knowledge, I do not have a single ancestor who was born or ever lived below the Mason-Dixon line.

Yet, here I am. And having lived over sixty years on southern soil, my heart, my soul, and my aging body are firmly planted, although admittedly, it took a number of years of cultivation to declare and defend the Southlands as my very own. And it was southern writers, along with my husband, his family, and friends, who helped me explore the intricacies and contradictions of their culture and gain a better understanding and greater appreciation of the complex legacy of my new homeplace.

To give a little background, my first experience living anywhere other than in California was in Stockholm, Sweden. My senior year in college, the year I turned twenty-one, I received an exchange scholarship from Occidental. In the 1950s foreign students on an American campus were a rarity and my college wanted to promote international understanding by bringing a Swedish girl to campus and sending me abroad. While in Europe, I met a man from Memphis, Tennessee. All I knew about Memphis at that time were Hoagy Carmichael's "shady verandas and Sunday blue skies." A year and a half later, I married that man from Memphis and moved to his hometown.

My cultural adjustment in moving from Bakersfield, California, to Memphis, Tennessee, was incredibly more challenging than my move from Los Angeles, California, to Stockholm, Sweden. Most of the nation, in fact most of the world, had very strong opinions about the South. While in Stockholm, one of my best friends was Barbara Levatt, a black girl from Boston. When she realized I was getting serious about that southern fellow I'd met on my Christmas holiday in Germany, she said, "Well, if you marry that man, I'll never come visit you." A black person from the North believed the South was a dangerous place. In fact, for many, it was.

Yet, from the very beginning, I realized that the South of the news reports and national journalists was very different from what I encountered. I, an outlier, was warmly welcomed by everyone I met—white and black. I felt immediately at home, even though I was bothered. The schools were segregated, there were separate drinking fountains for blacks and whites in public places, Thursday was Negro day at the Brooks Art Museum and the Memphis Zoo. However, for the sake of our new marriage, my husband and I declared a temporary moratorium on any discussion about race during those first few months, as he counseled me to get to know the people, both white and black.

I observed, listened, and learned of friends and dedicated leaders, both black and white, who were quietly working for change. Twelve years later, in April 1968, that leadership in three short days organized MEMPHIS CARES after Martin Luther King was assassinated in Memphis. Over six thousand people, black and white, poured into Crump stadium on a Sunday afternoon to pay tribute and show sorrow for the loss of that great man. It was a tense time. There had been violent demonstrations throughout the city the week before and my heart was in my throat as our young family walked the six blocks to the stadium to take our seats in the first totally integrated public gathering I had ever attended in the South.

During the preceding decade much of the larger southern culture had been violently torn asunder. The whole fabric of traditional southern life was tested, while at the same time I had faced a radical change in my own personal life. Our baby son was born in January of 1958; fifteen months later our first daughter was born; and in January of 1961, another baby daughter arrived. We had three babes under three for one day. During those next few years, I had lived within a personally constructed cocoon—protected, safe, very busy, and happy—as long, deep, festering fissures ripped apart my larger world.

In the summer of 1965, our young family had moved to a large, old house with two shady verandas. Our new-to-us, two-storied, stone and brick home with its original green tile roof was on a quiet street, lined by giant oaks in the heart of the Central Garden District of Memphis. Our house had been built in 1913, the same year the California town of Delano, my birthplace, had been incorporated. Somehow, that correlation gave graphic proof of how much my life had changed. Not only were these two places geographically distant—their living histories, though in the same nation, were distinctly very different.

One evening, after the children were upstairs tucked in bed for the night, I curled up on our living room sofa, eager to open Willie Morris's recently published, much touted book, *North Toward Home.* Mesmerized, I read deep into the night. Morris loved and cherished his roots in the South and being a southerner—his heritage, his people, the traditions, the food, the sports, the music, the landscape—yet he was brutally honest in claiming his deep ambivalence about the flaws and misdirection of those roots. Morris's words captured the strange, unsettling mass of my feelings toward my new life. Although the poet John Keats wrote, "Nothing ever becomes real till it is experienced," Willie Morris wrote, "Words are as important as experience, for words make an experience last." Often the words that capture and penetrate one's heart are words that describe experiences and feelings one has had but never expressed. Morris's words made me feel I belonged in the South.

It would be years before I felt the urge, or the courage, to try to pen my thoughts for others to read; however, in those years, I continued to listen. Someone once said that books provided a unique space for one to listen deeply. Even now, I am not a writer who easily writes about my own experience and feelings. I like to first listen and learn from others, before trying to assimilate and apply the truths they have ferreted out. Willie Morris and I were of the same generation. He was born in 1934. I was born in 1934. We were living through the same history, the same radio programs, the same presidents, the same music, the same wars. Someone once called us the silent generation—too late to be World War II heroes and just too early to be New Age firebrands.

Morris grew up in Yazoo City, a small country town like the one I'd known. Even though it was in a different part of our nation, many of his experiences and neighborhoods paralleled mine. His description of playing taps for the funeral of a fallen soldier of the Korean War in the cemetery on the Civil War battleground in Vicksburg touched me deeply, as I thought of my friend at East Bakersfield High School, who, in the summer before our senior year, enlisted in the Army to fight in Korea, was killed in action, and never returned home. Willie Morris's words helped me understand that with any relationship, even within myself, there are parts that lie in deep mystery, never to be exposed to the light of my knowing. But in the deepest of those unknowables lies the essence of being, of life, of love, of individuals, of place, and of a community.

After a mercurially successful literary career in New York City as a young man, Morris had rejected the "vapid life" of the intelligentsia and returned to his South. When Willie Morris died in 1991, his obituary in the *New York Times* said, "he never stopped exploring what in his own words he described as 'the warring impulses of one's sensibility to be both southern and American.'" Ralph Ellison, who felt much the same about the worthy aspects of Southern culture, was one of Morris's best friends. They both looked beyond the color of one's skin to discover an individual's character. Ellison's *The Invisible Man* was another of those incredible books I read about that time. I listened deeply and learned more and more of great goodness as well as horrible pain. Their words and those of other gifted southern writers were like scalding, circulating, Jacuzzi water against a tired, aching back. I began to relax and better understand my chosen homeland. And then there was Maya Angelou.

In the mid-1970s I was working in program development at the Meeman Center for Continuing Education of Southwestern (now Rhodes) College. Jim Lanier, a professor of history, Michael McLain, a professor of religion, and I applied for and received a grant from the Tennessee Committee for the Humanities to present a public symposium *SELF AND SOCIETY: Personal Identity in a Time of Change.* Eight nationally recognized scholars in the humanities were invited to give presentations in their particular area of expertise. Lanier and McLain were responsible for designing the program content and selecting the speakers, I was charged with the logistics and arrangements.

Maya Angelou was one of the presenters. At the time, I had never heard her name, seen her perform, or read anything she had written. But when Maya Angelou arrived in Memphis, I was swept into two of the most memorable days of my life by her warm, magnetic personality and magnificent presence. Six feet in height, she carried her large body with a dancer's grace. The deep, carefully enunciated, melodic resonance of her voice gave importance to her every word. It was not until later, when I read her book, *I Know Why the Caged Bird Sings,* that I understood why every word she spoke was so thoughtfully chosen. When she was eight years old, living in St. Louis, Maya Angelou was raped. When she told her brother the name of the man who had violated her, the man was arrested, tried in a court of law, but not convicted. Maya's family members later tracked him down and murdered him. She was devastated. This vivacious, smart little girl felt because she had spoken one word, his name, the man lost his life. Horrified with the power of her voice, with the power of her words, Maya swore to never speak again.

Maya Angelou became mute and was sent to live with her grandmother in Stamps, Arkansas. It was five years before she spoke another word, but while she was living in that small Negro community in Arkansas, a friend of her grandmother's invited this sad little girl to visit her daily. In the sanctity of Mrs. Bertha Flowers's home, Maya listened to this "elegant" older friend of her grandmother's read Shakespeare. Maya loved the sound, she loved the story, she loved the beat and cadence of the language. Gradually, very gradually, she began to write down and then recite some of the verses she had heard, while secreted behind the closed door of her bedroom, under her bed. Finally, when she was almost fifteen, having developed a deep appreciation for the music, sound, and meaning of the poetry, Maya Angelou once again began to speak aloud to others. The written and spoken word brought back her voice—brought back her life. Mrs. Bertha Flowers, with her southern grace, gave a frightened, mute child an extraordinary gift. Think of what Maya Angelou's life might have been if Mrs. Flowers of Stamps, Arkansas, had not invited that shame-filled little girl into her home every afternoon for nearly five years, to hear the beauty, rhythm, and wisdom of Shakespeare's words.

As a grown woman, remarkable artist, and human being, Maya Angelou constructed no barriers or distinctions based on skin color. She wanted her words, both written and spoken, to travel directly from heart to heart. After her visit to Memphis, those who met or heard her speak had felt an immediate connection.

Stories about and by southerners have shown me that good people, in spite of seemingly insurmountable problems and personal pain, spiritually, or perhaps organically, survive and grow through heart-to-heart connections—care and love for one's family, care and love for one's community, care and love for one's land, care and love for one's self, and care and love for the other, regardless of race or life station: Calpurnia's protective, no-nonsense care of Scout in Harper Lee's *To Kill a Mockingbird*; the power, grace, and responsibilities of the plantation mistress recorded by Thomas Nelson Page; the earthbound wisdom and honor of Cherokee tradition in Marilou Awiakta's *Selu*; the indomitable will of the pioneer women for establishing community described in Shirley Abbott's *Womenfolks*.

Being a woman, I readily and easily identify with the stories of women; but I also love stories of self-examination and the exploration of conflict, sadness, and rage in one's culture, in one's soul. Walker Percy's books are among my favorite. His search for *Love in the Ruins* or his quest for his southern soul *Lost in the Cosmos* show us over and over again that to live is to change. And only through an open heart can things change for the better, both personally and culturally. The more I read and deeply listened to the writings of southerners about the South, who so often express my thoughts better than I could express them myself, I realized, I am indeed a southerner—the South is where I belong.

III

Place, Politics, People

Southern writers have a great sense of place. That makes you write the truth. When you do that, people read it and say, "You wrote my life."
—MAGGIE BRITTON VAUGHN (POET LAUREATE OF TENNESSEE SINCE 1995)

Southern Fiction: A Tool to Stretch the Soul and Soften the Heart

Julie Cantrell

*M*y story begins in Louisiana, a land that gave me life—and, oh what a feral life it was! I begin my essay in the Bayou State because, for me, every story can be traced back to those densely tangled roots.

Many hear the word Louisiana and imagine a hot, humid mess of a place. They'd be correct. The humidity is fierce, the heat can be unbearable, and the air sometimes carries the odor of mud and fish, diesel engines and petroleum plants. On the surface it can appear a bit unpleasant if not downright threatening, especially in areas where litter is commonplace and poverty is extreme, where entire families reside in a shanty shack or an off-the-grid river camp or a rusty, gutted school bus surrounded by weeds.

But there is a reason native Louisianans rarely leave, and it's not because we're crazy—although most of us are and, truth be told, *normal* does not impress us much.

While Louisiana is indeed a hot mess of a state, lurking at the bottom of the map as a breeding ground for mosquitoes, alligators, nutria, and snakes, it is so much more than that. My homeland is an enchanted realm where sinners and saints meet beneath chapel spires, where voodoo lurks between tombstones, and where a casket can float right up out of the ground. It's a place where murky backwaters draw a darkness so deep, the only light comes from swamp gas or heat flash or early morning sea vessels.

We are a blended people in a land with blurred lines, a place thick with fog and back-alley jazz, where waters shift and levees break and the bayou itself can be heard breathing. It's a place where we stick together, even when we fall. A place where we come back swinging—or singing—no matter how many times life drags us under.

Louisiana is the only place in the world where someone can find a backyard crawfish boil, a Second Line parade, and a Sunday revival, all in the midst of fiddles, accordions, tubas, and trombones. It's a place of shotguns, airboats, and filé gumbo, not to mention a bag of beignets and a King Cake. Or two.

This Creole state is at once a fais do-do, a Mardi Gras, a baptism, and a cochon de lait. It's an early morning bateau aimed for trot lines or duck blinds. It's an old glass jug of cherry bounce or a whispered spell to keep the haunts at bay. It's a childhood spent in catechism or Sunday school, a calendar built around hunting seasons and offshore shifts. It's corrupt politicians, snake oil salesmen, mobsters, conmen, nuns, and priests, all gathered together for an SEC sunset on a Death Valley Saturday night.

Despite its rough edges and soiled soul, Louisiana is my heart's home, and I quite like it that way.

So what does Louisiana have to do with writing? Well, nothing. And everything.

At its beginning, the people who navigated these bayous were of two extremes. Either they were hired explorers out to stake a claim for some faraway king, or they were exiles kicked out of the more habitable lands until they reached the place where river meets sea. Once a home to native tribes, this boot-shaped state eventually became a land of misfits. A dwelling space for slaves, Gypsies, prisoners, refugees, and those on the run for reasons never told.

It sounds as if no one in their right mind would want to live here, but that's a far cry from truth.

Those of us who do share space with such ragged spirits would have it no other way. We are a people who take pride in doing life on our own terms, in placing our faith in something greater than ourselves, and being self-sufficient survivors. If there's anything I have learned from Louisiana, a shape-shifting state if ever there was one, it's that life will bring wave after wave of trauma and transition. Our job is to always, always, always find a way to adapt.

While Louisiana has long been a celebrated mix of cultures, ethnicities, religions, and class, undercurrents of bigotry do surface at times. I spent my childhood in a rural community, and in those days the few minorities who did reside in our town lived in one small section near the railroad tracks. It was called The Quarters, and I don't have to explain that name. Domestic violence was commonplace in our parish, and women—survivors in their own right—were often kept "in their place" by immature and/or insecure partners. Substance abuse played a big part in these abusive cycles, countered only by the evangelical teachings of absolute abstinence and the eternal wrath of God.

True to its roots, Louisiana remains a world of two extremes today. It is an all-or-nothing kind of world, reflected perfectly in the practice of Mardi Gras, a no-holds-barred carnival season followed immediately by the restrictive tradition of Lent. It's no wonder so few are able to maintain a steady balance in the midst of such chaotic swings.

As a child in Louisiana, I had to learn quickly how to navigate this wondrous place. It was all things wild and beautiful, at once pure and perilous. It was the kind of land where you keep your eyes wide open—for snakes, for spiders, for predators of all sorts.

Louisiana is about resilience, and any true Louisianian has learned that the hard way. One way I learned to survive such surroundings was by putting ink to page. As a young girl with bare feet and braids, I would climb into my backyard cedar tree and write in my journal. At first, I wrote about the world as I saw it. I wrote about the boys I wanted to marry, the love I had for my family, and the landscape that shaped my soul. But in time I began to write in greater detail about the people I loved, the people who formed my neighborhood, my community—and me.

I wrote about the man who gave his wife a black eye and then turned around to give us tomatoes from his garden. Another man who fed two stray puppies to the alligators before tossing the ball with us in the front yard. A woman who was drunk every afternoon by the time her kids got off the school bus, but who cooked her family three meals a day and packed her children's lunches every morning. A man who kept five pit bulls chained in the backyard for fighting, but who collapsed in tears when his young daughter was diagnosed with cancer. A woman who isolated herself after learning of her husband's affair, and the husband who continued to carry on as if nothing at all had happened, as if the whole wide world belonged to him.

As a child, I learned to pay attention, and I learned to process the crazy world around me by capturing it all on paper. I tackled adolescent angst by penning songs and melodramatic poetry. This led to gushy love letters, and a fair amount of thoughts about kissing. But I had no idea how therapeutic writing would become for me until I entered a high school literature class.

Our teacher assigned *To Kill a Mockingbird* by Harper Lee, and she required us to journal as if we were one of the characters from the story. Naturally, I chose Scout. I began writing as if I was this spunky, high-spirited little girl moving through a time and space I had never known. With that one assignment, writing became more than a way to document life around me. It became my favorite escape.

My journaling shifted in response. I no longer wrote *about* the people I observed. Instead, I began writing from the lens of each neighbor, relative, stranger, or friend. As I *became* the abusive husband, the alcoholic mother, the liar, the cheat, or the con, I began to unravel the complex dynamics that could lead any one of us into a particular place in life. It became clear that we were all just a few mistakes, mishaps, or choices away from one another, and I began to build a deep sense of empathy for every person whose path crossed mine—the good, the bad, and the ugly.

As that fourteen-year-old girl, I learned that fiction has the power to break down barriers. But it took me years to understand why. Now I believe fiction offers wide-open access to our emotional core, inviting us to draw from the well of truths that most of us have learned to avoid. When reading a nonfiction account of another person's experiences, we tend to enter that story with our defenses high. We may think to ourselves, "Oh, I'd never do that." Or "Wow, she's really selfish." Or "What an idiot!" It's easy for us to separate the real person's life from our own, and therefore we convince ourselves we could never end up in the trouble they're in because of x, y, or z.

This is an instinctive way to protect ourselves from the fear and anxiety that might arise if we dared consider someone else's messed-up life could very easily become *ours*. But it also prevents us from taking deep, honest glances at our own vulnerabilities and limits our opportunities for personal growth.

While nonfiction keeps us one step removed from the feelings, thoughts, and beliefs of another character, fiction tears down those walls. When we read fiction, we enter the story with an understanding that it is no threat to us because this situation is not real. In fact, it's never been real. And it never will be real. Not for the characters in the story, and certainly not for us.

Knowing these imaginary situations aren't likely to enter our actual lives, we can lower our defenses and fully walk in the skin of these characters without fear. This allows us to experience life through their lens and to identify with those who are "not like" us.

This is where the magic happens. By embracing a character's personal journey, we can begin to understand people who think differently, behave differently, and believe differently than we do.

Fiction builds empathy. Fiction is the truth teller. Fiction is the peacemaker.

And what does this have to do with the South? Louisiana is one small piece of the South, but it is a vital piece, and while many people may assume such a unique place can't possibly reflect their own communities, they'd be wrong. Louisiana reveals the human journey at its best and worst. On a larger scale, the South does the same.

In literature, the South works as a lure by tapping all the senses. When we set a story here, we not only deliver a cast of colorful characters, we share their sinful secrets while serving a mouth-watering meal. We draw readers in with soul-stirring music and landscapes that would make anyone want to disappear beneath the mossy oaks. The South offers a fantasy, a place where time slows and anxieties melt like the ice in a glass of sugar cane rum.

Readers of southern literature are invited to explore a place that exists on a level either above or below their own reality, even if they spend their actual lives right here with us in the South. Whether we draw a reader to the backwater bayous, the dusty Texas oil fields, or the misty Smoky Mountains, we pull them a world away from the nine-to-five grind, inviting them to climb aboard a Gulf Coast shrimp boat or take a stroll on a quiet Charleston boulevard. We drape them in feathers before parading them through the raucous crowds of Bourbon Street. We settle them into a shallow bateau or sway with them on a squeaking streetcar. We bring them out of their own worries and woes, and we allow them to become a different self. Then, with their defenses lowered, we are able to give them that invaluable new view, enabling them to end the book with a greater understanding of one another. And of themselves.

The South is the ideal setting for such soul exploration because it is not only alluring, it is complex. With complicated tensions, it would be easy to get caught in the trap of bigotry here. We all know hatred has destroyed many a soul in these parts. And beyond. But fiction allows us to avoid that undertow, to swim beyond the weight of such destructive beliefs. By stepping into a story, we learn to see the world from all sides, and we begin to realize we are all Louisianians. We are all just scrappy little souls doing the best we can to survive.

Many in life say the earth is our mother. If that's the case, then the South is the lap into which we all crawl to hear her story. It is the place where we learn a language of folklore and fairytales, happy-ever-afters and made-up myths. Here, swaddled in kudzu beneath the bower of magnolias, we nurse from the bosom of the universe's bard. We nestle snug in her arms, sipping on fables. We cut our teeth on plotlines, believing that we are the hero of her tales.

The South is nothing less than a sanctuary for story. It is the porch swing, the rocking chair, the barstool, the back pew. It is everything that made me and shaped me and saved me. As a southern writer, I aim only to invite my readers to enter this sacred space.

So to all I say, Welcome, welcome home. Life is hard and your soul is weary. Come in, kick off your shoes. You are safe here. Let me tell you a story.

The Burden of Southern Literature

Katherine Clark

A hundred years ago, anyone who contemplated writing serious literature about the South had to deal with what C. Vann Woodward famously called "the burden of southern history." By "burden," he meant that the history of the South after the Civil War stood in exact contrast to the history of America. Whereas the country at large was characterized by success of all kinds, the South was considered a defeated failure. America was a land of prosperity; the South was a region of poverty. As industrialization and urbanization swept the country, the South remained regressively rural and agricultural. The American self-image was one of moral superiority and idealism, while the South had harbored the original sin of slavery. In his essay, "The Search for Southern Identity," Woodward presents a series of these stark contrasts between the collective experience of America as opposed to that of the South.

The burden for a would-be writer in the South 100 years ago was the fear that no one either inside or outside the region would want to read about a place marred by failure, poverty, slavery, backwardness, and a horde of social, political, and economic side effects. If the South was a national embarrassment and a pocket of shame, what reader would be drawn to this subject matter? And if the South was so different from the rest of the country, why would most Americans want to read about something that did not connect or relate to them? So at the beginning of the twentieth century, there was no such thing as a "southern writer." There were writers in the South searching for subjects that would strike a chord with a national audience.

William Faulkner was one of these authors. At the beginning of his career, he had no intention of writing about "the South." His first novel was about a soldier returning from World War I to put his life back together in a small Georgia town. (But Georgia—where Faulkner had never lived—was not the point.) His second novel was about the bohemian society in New Orleans, where he lived for a time. It was while in New Orleans that Faulkner had an epiphany courtesy of his fellow writer Sherwood Anderson, whom Faulkner credits with teaching him that his own "postage stamp of native soil" was worth writing about. In his third novel, *Flags in the Dust* (originally published as *Sartoris*), Faulkner writes for the first time about his mythical Yoknapatawpha County in Mississippi.

Faulkner's epiphany became a collective one for an entire generation of authors in the South, who learned to embrace the distinctiveness of their cultural heritage instead of shying away from it. If the South was so different from the rest of the country, then a southern novel could be fascinating for a reader who had never been there. It would be like a trip to an exotic location. If the southern experience was so different from mainstream America, then a novel about the South could have much to teach the rest of the country. These are the realizations that paved the way for the southern literary renaissance.

Now, at the beginning of the twenty-first century, the writer in the South is not plagued by the burden of southern history, but by the burden of southern literature. Our literary tradition is revered all over the world and has produced many of the best writers to come out of our country. Southern literature is the strongest tradition in American literature, and one of the greatest gifts that American culture has given to the world. But for the writer in the South today, southern literature is both a blessing and a curse. It has inspired us and it has educated us, but it can also intimidate us into either silence or imitation. We can be so overwhelmed by the shadow of Faulkner, Flannery O'Connor, Eudora Welty, Tennessee Williams, James Agee, Harper Lee, and so many others that we either never find our own voice, or resort to some form of echoing these early great voices which forged our literary heritage.

When I first started out, I thought I *needed* to echo my forebears in order to be a successful "southern writer." Consequently, I felt shortchanged by growing up amidst a wealthy, well-educated, suburban population in an exclusive enclave of the post–Civil War industrial city of Birmingham. *Nothing* about my background was in keeping with the settings I found in great southern fiction. If I wanted to be a true southern writer, I believed I couldn't write about my own city of Birmingham or community of Mountain Brook, which I also found boring and sterile anyway. My doubts were confirmed by a professor in graduate school who flatly told me that I could never be a true southern writer because I didn't come from a small town. This professor's claim to fame was the interview he'd once conducted with the Great Man Faulkner himself, and even when I learned that Faulkner had hated this professor and his article so much that he actually named a dog after him so he could kick it, my doubts remained about my credentials to write true southern fiction.

Then there was the box of family memorabilia my aunt gave me because I was "the writer" in the family. This box contained a treasure trove of newspaper clippings, letters, cards, and photographs focusing on our illustrious Alabama ancestor who'd enlisted in the Civil War as a poor seventeen-year-old private from a subsistence farm near Scott's Mill in the northern part of the state. Wounded in the battle of Chickamauga, he lost a leg and spent three years in a Yankee prison in Atlanta. An Atlanta *Journal-Constitution* clipping told the story of his sister, who, as a spy for Nathan Bedford Forrest, had the use of a horse, which she rode 300 miles to visit her brother in prison. When the war ended, she rode back and brought him home.

The one-legged Jesse Edward Brown earned his law degree, became a member of the Alabama State Legislature, helped transform Scott's Mill into a county seat renamed Scottsboro, and in the process became a wealthy landowner. As a result of his wealth, status, and missing leg, he was addressed as "Colonel" and revered as a war hero, although he'd never been more than a private and spent most of the war in a prison. When he died, General Joseph Wheeler wrote a note of condolence to his widow.

Now this was Faulkner territory. This was the novel I needed to write. So for years I tried my best to do it. But I couldn't. I had never known Scottsboro when my family's renowned Brownwood estate hosted horse races every Sunday, which hundreds of people from three states came to watch. I did not spend summers there, as my father did, and had no knowledge of my small-town relatives or their community. Lacking any visceral connection to the southern past captured in that box of memorabilia, I was unable to bring it to life in the pages of a novel. And I was always haunted by the certainty that precisely because this was Faulknerian material, I had nothing to offer compared to what he'd already created.

Often I encounter southern novels that try to do what I tried for years to do with my box of family mementos, and I recognize in these works the same pitfalls that obstructed my efforts. In these novels, the quirks of southern culture and the tropes of southern literature are all-too-eagerly deployed and milked to the very last drop. One novel I read a few years ago contained incest, miscegenation, faith healing, a lynching, a KKK cross-burning, a race riot, and childbirth without benefit of hospital or doctor. I felt like the author had started out with a checklist. If novels like this had an accent, it would be an overdone southern drawl from a B movie.

Whereas 100 years ago, writers had to learn to embrace the differences of the South, nowadays the tendency can be to positively wallow in the eccentricities and grotesqueries of the southern experience, *usually of an earlier era.* This is what the southern novel needs to save itself from. We shouldn't be wallowing in southern-ness, and we don't even need to embrace it either, because that's been done. That's a given now, thanks to our great literary ancestors. Our job today is not to stick to the foundation they laid for us, but to use it as a springboard launching us in the new and different directions demanded by a changing culture.

But it is not easy to labor in the shadow of a great literary tradition—to try to live up to it and also add to it. The Southern Renaissance generation encountered virgin territory that they laid claim to and were the first to develop in serious literature. They had a blank slate that writers in the South today do not have. If twenty-first-century authors in the South want to succeed, we have to be mindful of how crowded that slate has become. We have to study what's on it, not only to learn from it, but to figure out what part of it remains undeveloped, and what kind of structures have not been built. We have to identify our own space and fill it with something original. In a sense, we need different tools for our different task. Whereas the shock value of the South's uniqueness served that first generation of southern writers very well, today's writers are better served by subtlety.

Ironically, I think I finally became a "southern writer" when I stopped trying to be one and started writing a novel not about my Confederate forebear, but about my high school English teacher. In this novel, my mission was not to write about "the South" at all, but to capture the character of an extraordinary individual who was such a major influence on so many people's lives that he impacted an entire community. In the process of depicting this community, I was forced to write about Mountain Brook. To provide context for that, I was forced to write about Birmingham.

This is when my awakening occurred. As embarrassing and even ridiculous as it is to admit, this is when I realized that my own postage stamp of native soil was my community of Mountain Brook and my city of Birmingham. It took me decades to see something that was right in front of me, staring me in the face. But just as that earlier generation of authors had to learn to embrace differences between the South and the rest of the country, I had to learn to embrace the difference between my postage stamp and the one usually found in classic southern literature. This epiphany also involved an awareness that self-conscious southernism is a recipe for cliché and bad writing. I put myself on the path to writing a decent southern novel only when I stopped trying to write a "southern novel" and was simply trying to write an original novel set in the South. This is the main lesson I learned from years of struggling to be a southern writer, and the main pearl of wisdom I have for anyone engaged in the same struggle.

When I first started graduate school at a university in the South after four years of college in the Northeast, I was so overly enthusiastic about returning to my southern roots that one of my professors—not the one Faulkner liked to kick through his dog, but another professor—put the brakes on this excess with a word of advice. "Please don't turn into a professional southerner," he warned me. These are words to live by for anyone who aspires to be a southern writer.

In the Land of Cotton

John M. Floyd

outhern fiction. What's the big deal about it? Why in the world do so many readers seem to be fascinated by stories written or set in locations south of the Mason-Dixon? And why has this area of the country produced so many authors?

Well, I have a few views on that. I'll admit I'm biased; except for a stint in the Air Force and some far-flung travels during my career with IBM, I've spent my whole life in what is arguably the heart of the Deep South, and I love it. My homeland is a strange and special place.

The fact is, things are just *different* down here, and not all those things are good. Everyone knows about our history and our struggles and our social issues—but if you live here you also know what strides we've made in the past fifty years or so. Do we still have problems? You bet we do. But some of those same problems exist in the Midwest and New England, and on both coasts.

I've always suspected that we might owe our rich literary heritage, at least to some degree, to those problems. After all, how can one write convincingly about conflict and pain and failure if he's never seen them firsthand, or at least seen their consequences? The South has always been a place of contrasts: wealth/poverty, hospitality/prejudice, stability/volatility. I will admit that I have lived a fairly sheltered life, but I've still seen the extremes, and I know people well who live on both ends of the socioeconomic ladder. And I think the literature that comes out of such a diverse culture will sometimes show greater intensity and emotion. According to Alabama author Rick Bragg: "We are good at stories. We hoard them, like an old woman in a roomful of boxes, but now and then we pull out our best, and spread them out. We talk of the bad years when the cotton didn't open, and the day my cousin Wanda was washed in the blood. We buff our beloved ancestors until they are smooth of sin, and give our scoundrels a hard shake, although sometimes we can't remember who is who."

Perhaps the biggest reason for the abundance of authors from the South, however, is this: southern kids grow up listening to a lot of different people *tell* stories. Or at least they used to, when I was a boy. Our storytellers were relatives, friends, relatives of friends, friends of relatives, old-timers, co-workers, you name it. Some were folks we had never seen before in our lives and would never see again—nameless wanderers who happened to stop by for a glass of iced tea or a plate of food on their way to points unknown. Those vagabonds would now be called homeless persons, but back then we knew them only as hoboes, which to us meant adventurers who had traveled the globe and seen things we could only dream about. I can recall sitting at their feet beside the bench in front of my grandfather's gas station in Sallis, Mississippi, wide-eyed and gullible and marveling at their tales while they munched Nabs and Tom's Toasted Peanuts and sipped RC Colas bought for them by my granddad from the Coke machine inside the hot but shaded office. Most of their thrilling accounts, I realize now, were pure fiction—but I can remember some of them to this day.

Did those stories influence me to later tell my own tall tales? Of course they did—especially my short small-town mysteries and their laid-back style. Did they make me a *good* storyteller? Maybe not. But they made me want to *be* a good storyteller. And the odds are with me: My native Mississippi is the birthplace of more published authors per capita than any other state, and the Delta town of Greenville has produced more published authors than any other *city* in the nation. If I don't make it, it's no one's fault but my own.

Another factor in the South's production and development of authors is, I believe, the fact that we grew up among such colorful characters. Almost everyone seemed to have a hidden past, or a flair for the dramatic, or at least a mischievous gleam in his eye. And I'm referring to women as well as men, here. I recently heard my cousin say, after she'd been told that it would probably be illegal to fire a gun at a trespasser unless he was inside her house at the time, that if the situation arose she would by God shoot him in her yard and then drag his body into the house before the police arrived. And speaking of folks being "colorful," it's a little surprising to recall how many of my parents' friends had nicknames—the southeastern United States is a great place for nicknames. Within several miles of my hometown lived men and women who were known only as Jabbo, Biddie, Pep, WeeWee, Buster, Puddin', Doo-spat, Ham, Big 'un, Nannie, Bobo, Snooky, and Button. How could folks with those kind of names be anything *but* interesting?

And, yes, it must be said: some of our old acquaintances go beyond "interesting." Some venture into the area of eccentric, weird, and even outrageous. "Whenever I'm asked why southern writers have a penchant for writing about freaks," Flannery O'Connor once said, "I say it is because we are still able to recognize one."

The truth is, no one really knows, or will ever know, why this region has been home to so many wordsmiths. I just know it has. I even wish there had been *more* Faulkners and Weltys and Grishams and Conroys and Tennessee Williamses in the world. And maybe there will be.

I also know this: In my travels I've been inside bookstores all across the nation, and I have yet to see a section labeled "Northern Fiction." Maybe that, in itself, is revealing.

Good or bad, and with or without its many literary alumni, the South is a unique world. It's a place with a deep commitment to family, to community, to religion. A place where most folks still respect their elders, say grace before meals, have at least one relative named Bubba, and feel free to drop in for an unannounced visit at anybody's house at any time. (Except maybe my pistol-packin' cousin's.)

One more point. Some southern authors—Nevada Barr, Cormac McCarthy, and others—were born elsewhere but have lived and written here in kudzu country for many years. One might say they're southern by choice rather than southern by blood.

As for me, I'm both. I love it here, and God willing, I'll never leave.

Matter of fact, I think I feel a story coming on. . . .

Where I Write

Jennifer Horne

*I*n grade school we wrote our addresses on a piece of lined paper in careful handwriting:

> Jennifer Horne
> 2020 N. Arthur
> Little Rock
> Pulaski County
> Arkansas
> The United States
> North America
> The World
> The Solar System
> The Milky Way
> The Universe.

The address extended outward into something called infinity. The closest I could get to understanding infinity was by considering the number of books in the world, starting with the tall, packed shelves in the large, sunlit room that was the children's section of the Little Rock Public Library. How would I ever read them all? Gertrude Stein once said that her greatest fear was running out of books, which like infinity is hard to imagine.

Growing up, I had no notion that other Americans lived any differently from how we did. I was aware of some prejudices against Arkansans in particular and southerners in general. People from elsewhere thought we talked funny and found it humorous to parody our accents. Once on vacation in

Florida a boy expressed surprise that people from Arkansas were wearing shoes—or maybe he was just tease-flirting. I was never very good at figuring that out. I knew that the episodes of *The Beverly Hillbillies* we watched after school presented a comical portrait of the "poor mountaineer" Jed Clampett and his backwoods family from an unspecified place in the Ozarks, but it never occurred to me that we'd be mistaken for them. The 1957 Central High desegregation crisis defined Arkansas for many, but with the insouciance of youth I believed such things were now in the past, playing as I did on an integrated softball team and being bused to integrated schools. At Episcopal church camp I kissed a black fellow camper. What I didn't know to see I just didn't see.

For many years now my address has been Canyon Lake, Cottondale, Alabama, and so on out to The Universe. After Alabama and before The United States, however, I'd now add "The South." I've lived and traveled outside of the South and even created a college class on foreign travelers' perspectives on the region over two centuries, and I have come to understand I grew up somewhere different, a hunter's stew of history and hope and horror. And however much scholars assert that the South is losing its distinctive qualities due to mass media, greater mobility, fast food, and chain stores, writing from this place—even feeling the need to say that I write *from a place*—has an effect on the way I write.

In *A Portrait of the Artist as a Young Man*, James Joyce's Stephen Dedalus also writes his address, in his geography book: "Stephen Dedalus, Class of Elements, Clongowes Wood College, Sallins, County Kildare, Ireland, Europe, The World, The Universe." Joyce found it impossible to write in Ireland, or to write what he wanted in the face of religious restrictions on free speech and an oppressively moralistic culture, and he went all the way to Trieste to find his freedom. Trieste, Zurich, Paris—exotic names to conjure up a writer's life. Joyce speaking as Stephen says: "I will tell you what I will do and what I will not do. I will not serve that in which I no longer believe, whether it call itself my home, my fatherland or my church: and I will try to express myself in some mode of life or art as freely as I can and as wholly as I can, using for my defence the only arms I allow myself to use—silence, exile, and cunning."

Just out of college I had a fantasy of moving to New York City and living among the bohemians of the Chelsea Hotel. Instead, I did the practical thing: I moved to Missouri and enrolled in a master's program in journalism. Many southern-born writers—I think of Willie Morris and *North Toward*

Home—have exiled themselves from their home places in order to survive, economically or psychically, or simply to gain the distance necessary to see their place clearly enough to write about it. Others, and I count myself among them, stay. But I think of my home in the woods with my husband as a place apart, and of my study there as yet another step of separation. It is my place of internal exile, where exile is a place chosen, a place of thinking freely. The roots of the word *exile* speak of banishment, imply being driven out to wander the roads. And the word *banish* is connected through its roots to bandit, to being outlawed or, say, to claiming outlaw status. Because no matter how much I enjoy setting a pretty table or engaging in the niceties of southern politeness at the grocery store, no matter that I still believe in thank-you notes and eat black-eyed peas on New Year's Day, being a writer makes me an outlaw, and this is my hideout.

I write in a twenty-by-forty-foot space with an outside deck like the prow of a ship. At one end is a wall of books, floor to ceiling. At the deck end is a repurposed sliding glass door that serves as a window to the woods beyond. A daybed sits there for naps and contemplation. The windows on one long side look toward the lake, on the other toward the woods. This is the last place I say goodbye to when leaving the house on trips, the first place I greet returning. I sometimes fear fire and calm myself by remembering that writers Rita Dove and Fred Viebahn survived a fire at their house, and so I could too. They even learned to dance afterwards.

Talismans, large and small, surround me: the oak wardrobe that belonged to my great-grandfather, who moved it from north Alabama to Arkansas, where it ended up on my grandmother's back porch painted blue, where my mother rescued it, stripped and refinished it, and eventually bequeathed it to me, who moved the great bulk of it and the poem my mother wrote about it from Arkansas to Missouri and back to Alabama. It's come full circle, as stories sometimes do. Family photos, two framed embroidered trees (one by me, one by my mother), thrift-store art finds, Arkansiana, the last chair from my grandmother's dining room suite—almost every object, and there are many, has a story attached, and when I look up from reading or writing I feel comforted by their presence and, often, prompted to some chain of recollection by whatever my eye alights upon. Once when we were looking for paper to draw on, my then seven-year-old grandson stood in this room, gazed around taking it all in, and said, "This must have taken a long time to decorate." Well, yes. Lifetimes.

For all the writers who've found the anonymity of the coffee shop or the hotel room conducive to working, there must be another bunch of us who revel in familiarity. Touring Eudora Welty's house in Jackson, I felt the settledness of her place, the views and smells and creaks in the floorboards that tell you you're home, that this is where you write from. It's a safe place for dreaming, and even a place for daring, for, as Welty says so eloquently at the end of *One Writer's Beginnings*, "all serious daring starts from within." And, of course, it's that "room of one's own" that Virginia Woolf advocated for. Although I first read Woolf's essay decades ago, I've felt a particular connection to it ever since I discovered that the subject of my current book project, Alabama-born writer Sara Mayfield, had tea with Virginia Woolf while living in London in the late twenties and wrote home the next day that Woolf "is working on a book in which she contends that women would be as creative as men, perhaps, if they had fixed incomes and a room of their own in which to work. To which, I say, Amen!" We jokingly speak of my study as the Jennifer Horne Poetry Wing (sometimes, prematurely, the Jennifer Horne Memorial Poetry Wing) because we built it after I moved into my husband's house and discovered I needed much more room to work in than a desk in the guest bedroom. (And yes, I feel I need a guest bedroom, too.) This house, starting as a two-room weekend cabin in the 1940s, has been added onto and added onto, and, who knows, may be yet again. To be able to expand, to breathe as needed is one thing my place has given me.

I have two desks, one on each long wall, each facing windows. One might be thought of as the prose desk, the other as the poetry desk. One is connected to the outside world via the internet, the other connects to what is immediately outside via windows, lower-case w. At the prose desk (a dark wood door set on filing cabinets) are my laptop, printer, stacks of notes for current projects. At the poetry desk (a refectory-style table my mother found at a used furniture store on 9th Street in downtown Little Rock) are my folders of poems, stacks of old writing notebooks and journals with writing ideas, and a few of the smaller talismans: an antique vase painted with flowers and a windmill, a silvery raku-glazed goblet I made in a pottery class, a compass, a scallop shell, a Walter Anderson painting on a postcard (a man rowing, facing backwards in order to move forward), a brick from the demolished Kwik-Snak restaurant in Tuscaloosa where I met for coffee with writer friends in graduate school, the doorknob I took from the house (it was being renovated at the time) where Zelda painted in the Asheville asylum. The prose desk is for typing, the poetry desk for writing by hand. For a while recently the poetry desk languished. I realized I had made of it a tableau, the way suburban southern front porches these days tend to have rocking chairs that no one sits in, conveying only the idea of porch life. I didn't like conveying (to myself) only the idea of writing, so I cleared and wiped down the poetry desk and set about using it for all kinds of handwriting, from poems to the aforementioned thank-you notes to lists of lists I need to make to the beginnings of stories. I look out the window at the lake and consider it a good omen when a great blue heron lopes by, if a flying thing can be said to lope. There's usually one of my two brown dogs lying nearby, keeping me company, which means there's usually some dog hair floating around. I'd rather write or read than vacuum or dust, and a houseful of books and papers is not conducive to housecleaners, as comedies about important papers being reshuffled or tossed out from "tidying up" attest. And honestly, I'm disinclined to have someone in, as in my limited experience you have to clean the house to have the house cleaned. Growing up in Little Rock there were still phalanxes of black women in white uniforms who came daily or weekly to many of the houses of my friends, and at times to mine, à la *The Help*. That dynamic has finally shifted, and many of the people I know who employ a housekeeper now employ Hispanic women, recently arrived in the US. I wonder what new stories this change will birth. Will there be any equivalent to Howell Raines's Pulitzer Prize–winning "Grady's Gift"? How will these women working hard to make better lives for themselves and their children change the Old South dynamic, the often uneasy *noblesse oblige* of the employing classes?

My study is geographically located in Alabama but psychologically apart from its churches on every corner, its conservative politics, its fascination with football, its pressure to conform as it pretends to treasure its eccentrics. As a writer I am in and of the South but also apart from it, more or less passing as I go about my daily life, eavesdropping, spying even, standing a little off to the side and taking mental notes, trying to do so with empathy and understanding, because it is only by remaining enough of an insider to be a part of things that I can report on what goes on around me with the human voice a reader recognizes as revealing rather than judging.

I've thought about this question of passing and whether it's cowardly. I am a middle-class white woman in midlife. I don't sport tattoos or put blue streaks in my hair or wear clothes that stand out in a crowd. Will I wear my

trousers rolled? Do I dare to eat a peach? Am I a cautious Prufrock in Alabama, avoiding action, allowing people I disagree with to think I share their
convictions in order to minimize conflict? Sometimes I am. But sometimes
I speak up, out loud and on the page, because other voices need to be heard.
And nontraditional perspectives can come from surprising quarters. Once
in a book group sponsored by the campus Episcopal church in Tuscaloosa,
the minister asked, Socratically, what happened to us when we died. There
was a pause as everyone thought about the proper theological response, and
then one of the older ladies said, in a moment of honesty and clarity, "I think
people remember us after we're gone." Not a word about Heaven.

I want inclusion, not division, and I want my words to provoke without
creating so much distance between me and my readers that they turn off.
Seeking words that say more about who I am as I move about in this world,
I've accumulated bumper stickers and T-shirts. My bumper stickers say "I
Love the Tuscaloosa Public Library," "Support the Arts," and "Wag More,
Bark Less." The T-shirts proclaim: I ♥ NPR, PBS, Well-Behaved Women
Rarely Make History, Art *Is* Education, Hide Away in a Good Book, and a Dr.
Seuss–inspired "I Will Read Books on a Boat. . . ." The NPR shirt came first,
after I heard of a nice, respectable doctor in town referring to it as Nigger
Public Radio. It's the rare doctor's office in my town that does not have Fox
News blaring on the mounted television set. It's assumed that's what most
people will want to watch.

I have such ambivalence about this region that I write from. How do I
critique with a loyal heart? How do I claim this ambivalence? Or, as people
sometimes ask me when I complain, which I do, why stay? Partly for the usual
reasons of connections and convenience, partly for the place I've found in the
literary community across my state and region, partly, even, because a certain
amount of creative energy is generated by pushing against the dominant
culture. But also because it's my right to belong here, to cheer the small-town
art museum, to talk to the little girl at the book signing who says she has so
much more she'd like to say about poetry but she has to go to choir practice,
and to be open to the serendipitous moment when the predictable becomes
radical, whimsical, inexplicably open. I go to get my hair cut just down the
road, and when my hairdresser asks me what's new, I take a chance and tell
her I have a book of poems just out, and she tells me she remembers enjoy-
ing *The Canterbury Tales* in high school and recites the opening lines. It's in
those moments I realize that I can change my perspective on the place I live

simply by showing more of who I am, and in the process making space for others to show who they are, beyond the conventional, made-up face they present to the world. I stay here to continue to insist, as the saying goes, that y'all means all, that the loudest, crudest voices don't get to have the last word.

Oh, I could move to a liberal enclave in the no-nonsense North, but I like a bit of nonsense, the playful linguistic meander down a silly conversational byway that can happen with stranger or friend alike, the shared acknowledgment of the perplexing absurdity of life that seems a lot more likely to happen here than elsewhere.

That's What *She* Said:
The Sordid Business of Writing

Suzanne Hudson with RP Saffire

I am a very recent, unfashionably reticent arrival at The Facebook, having finally caved after years and years of being told that "you *have* to be a presence" on social media in order to have any hope whatsoever of being noticed as an author. Okay. Uncle. Unfortunately, if personal history is any indication, my tardy attendance in cyber-world will likely be just in time to see the morphing of the FB cyber into the next Trendy Trend. I'm typically the last one to the cyber party, just as the drunken guests are calling it a night. Clearly my social/business/sales acumen is not cutting edge; I'm just not wired that way. Hell, I was five years into this authoring thing before I realized what "networking" meant, and it wasn't pretty.

But Facebook has not been disappointing. I've avoided those pockets of "mean girl" juju, where grown humans devolve to their fifth-grade selves, and I discovered intriguing, funny, informative folks and places that plug into the curious and positive places within me. Just the other week I was reading an interesting string of posts on the author Cris Mazza's page. She had posed a question about writers' photos on book jackets. Did women have different experiences from men regarding how "serious" or "distinguished" to look (as opposed to smiling, for example)? Were "props" (kittens, glasses, whatevers) encouraged or not? Was there any generalized sexism going on? One of the commenters noted that packaging, marketing, et al. was a "game," that the author should simply play the game if he/she wanted to win. And here Cris posited, warming the cockles of my heart: "I wonder, what does one 'win' in art?"

We are, after all, making art here.

I know a few visual artists who are of the mind that painters, for example, should not sign their work; the very act of signage cheapens, degrades the purity of the art. My husband, author Joe Formichella, tends to agree, claiming that true literary art would make itself evident; the style of the author would be recognizable—if it were distinctive, good enough. And I get it. I taught in the public school system and could recognize, if voices were unique enough, who wrote what, and when Little Johnny plagiarized and when the secretary had written an email for the principal to send out as his/her own. It is a simple (complex?) question of style, which is borne up by "process," that overly analyzed, squirm-worthy word.

But of course we all ponder it. For example, I know my writing "process" well enough to know that I will not be able to even think about beginning to be fixin' to put fingertip to keyboard unless my physical environment is in order—not perfect, not "finished," as that is not possible—but on some weird, obsessive level I must have the world in which I am immediately ensconced orderly *enough* to make the mental leap into the land of word-wielding. I must finish painting this, cleaning that, filing the other, or striking a list before the current manuscript, which is, yes, fermenting in my head, can begin its slow ooze onto the page.

It seems that my actual mental "process," too, requires a cleansing purge, to open the way toward verbal clarity. In fact, the first essay I submitted for this anthology was met with dismay by a panel of readers, two of whom used descriptors like "off-putting," "unpleasant," and "angry"; that it was reflective of my "current unhappiness"; and a "misappropriated opportunity" to impart helpful wisdom to fledgling writers. I admit that my hackles rose up and my little bitty feelings were hurt—for about thirty seconds. It was that fast that I knew the editors/readers were absolutely correct. There had been a mighty boil of rage and hurt amassing in my spirit for a couple of years, and that sucker had to be lanced and drained of the pus of bitterness, pain, and betrayal before I could even think about what to really, honestly—and calmly—write.

Purge accomplished.

So what now to impart? I instinctively shy away from academic analyses, literary references, author quotes, and comments on the canon, preferring to leave that to the academics, them there folks what's got them fancy degrees and all. I'm intimidated by such.

I resist offering advice on when and how and why to proceed, having realized that so many aspiring writers (including myself) desperately seek rules, a framework, a set-in-stone—yes, that word again—"process," when there are no rules, no absolutes, nothing to know except one sure thing that one must have: a damn good editor.

As for the "process" of putting out a product/book, the world of publishing has changed so dramatically in the last half-dozen years that the bad old days of authors cum publicists cum salesmen—and even publishers—seem to be winding down. To that I say, "Hallelujah!"

In order to illustrate what I mean, allow me to introduce you to one RP Saffire, a semi-alter ego of mine, a brassy broad who is in your face, overly confident, verbally ornate, defiant of rules, and determined to be the next Great American Writer, until she has her own moment of clarity, when she realizes that, hey, fame and recognition ain't the freakin' point. Her nonfiction book, *Second Sluthood, Second E-dition* is the second iteration of *Being a Manifesto for the Post-Menopausal, Pre-Senilic Matriarch*, which recounts her foray into literary/author world, from paid advice at book festivals to a demented writing workshop professor to the inevitable world of business and marketing, which, in the last half of the twentieth century, glommed onto too many of the true creative spirits amongst us, and with devastating results. Yep, there are soul-killing consequences to art when the profit motive sets in.

But I should let her speak for herself. Here is what *she* said, when she first inhabited my body, just after the century's turn:

JUNE 6, 2003

I put my heart here before you, kind strangers, in the hope that you will nurture it, tend to the chambers and valves of its creative spirit, resist the urge to bypass it or shun(t) it or inject it with the purple dye of your disdain, and simply respond with tenderness. Just Try a Little.

You see, I am a writer.

I am over fifty.

Of late I have been wanting to be "published"—validated, as it were, by the minions of the mega-millionaires who decide what you beings out there ingest into your cerebral cortexes. Ah, you might say that you alone select what you read, and well you should, yet it is all predetermined by those business men and women who study the bottom line, who package their book writers in Back Street Boys cynicism, and who purchase real estate along the Boardwalks and Park Places in every bookstore chain in the land. Yet and still, I have sought out said book writers.

And lo, I say unto you, I have followed the wisdom handed down by those anointed ones who have the advantage of corporate validation, having had their egos salved with the ointment of ad men and publicists (whose own egos were most certainly primed with greased palms, so to speak). They are called "authors." A distinctive word, since the world is filled with writers and wanna-be writers. My manicurist is writing a book, as is my neighbor, my florist, and the cashier at the corner Mini-Mart. Everyone else *wants* to write a book, because, however unremarkable, dull, and boorish they are, they really do believe they have something like a shot at being entertaining, or better yet, famous. And with the increasing incidences of unpolished self-publishing, there is a tidal wave of written trash trending in ripples from your second cousin once removed to big, profitable splashes of poorly written, hollow character-inhabited jaw droppers of excuses for real literature. Them folks ain't authors.

An *author* is a writer who has been published, designated "legit" by the industry, edited and promoted, thus becoming akin to something like a holy one, larger than life—like Gandhi, say, or the Pope, or Oprah. I have listened to these gods, demigods, and semi-gods at conferences, seen them in person, out of person (as in on Book TV and the like), via magazines and National Public Radio. I have gone through demoralizing, failed attempts at making those oh so very critical "connections" the Holy Ones discuss, "connections" which actually involve puckering up one's Revloned lips and connecting them to someone's divine derriere. I have kissed perfumed asses, pimply asses, hairy asses, and flaccid asses—all figuratively, of course. I have sent the odometer on my Mustang convertible spinning like the window-paned panel of a Gulf Coast slot machine, handsomely boosting the profits of the oil industry as I drive from conference to conference all around the Southeast, even venturing forth to Chicago, New York, Washington, D.C., and . . . nothing. What was once a heaving hunger within my voluptuous bosom has become a deflated implant, leaking a poisonous, siliconic sap into my sagging spirits.

I have come back to writing in the midst of a second life that, combined with the afterglow of menopause, gives me the attitude of nothing short of an *uber*-heroine, a mouthpiece for those females among us who have arisen from such ashes, such incineration as we never in a million years expected or even suspected, in our wide-eyed youth, might be awaiting our fragile frames. I have returned to my core, my . . . *self,* after a lifetime of being in the dead zone of a charade of a marriage and, in a meaningless moonlit career (to subsidize my daylight job as a teacher with the pittance-paying public school system, yet another nightmare scenario) as a real estate agent on the coast: Gulf Shores, Alabama, the Redneck Riviera.

My childhood friend (and re-birthed Christian) Opal insists that nothing short of a blog will cement my installation into the literary landscape, that tapping out short messages to an ocean of unseen souls is critical in the twenty-first-century lay of the net. Opal has had web-cam experiences that make an agnostic like me blush, but her wealth of experience in that realm—that of the web—must surely count for something.

And so it begins, this maiden voyage into the net with this, my first blog entry.

At which point I, Ruby Pearl Saffire, wordsmith extraordinaire, gave up on the whole bloggy endeavor.

Opal was as frustrated with me as I was frustrated with the traversing of the nets. Clearly I was not cut out for techno-world. Ergo, a book. A real life, hold-it-in-your-hands, smell-the-pages book, aimed at ladies of a certain age and even ladies just coming of age—validation for the former, and wisdom/warning/guidance for the latter. A Matriarchal Manifesto of twenty-seven rules for living the slutty life, along with poetry, self-help, and a bit of social commentary. From the tattered tapestry of my experiences I would offer an alternative path back to desire. From the dull frost of frigid goals, I would offer the shine of creativity, like the facets of an indigo sapphire against vulval verbosity, the most cunning of linguistical conclusions.

My literary blooming commenced. I struck out—slowly—into the world of writing, to the occasional conference or book fest, only to strike out in the finding of any inroad into the publishing world. Alas, the vast majority of agents and owners and editors were not looking for raw talent with which to build a body of work, to guide and nurture and groom into a towering figure of great literature, to be studied for succeeding generations as a purveyor of universal truths. I admit to doing a little nosedive at the realization that here was yet another non-verdant façade, that money and celebrity had infiltrated the pristine beauty of the well-written word. Everywhere were hawkers and hacks and egos and prima donnas. No talent abounded, and the almighty dollar ruled the day.

The dream had become a lie.

I can feel the incredulity of those readers who might have made the attempt to write for publication, the ones who prowl the book conferences watching for crumbs to fall into their ink-stained palms, the Stigmata of the un-chosen ones. It is a little-known subculture, this legion of would-be literati who ebb and flow behind the literary scene, who do not yet realize that personal power can be easily seized once any particular person ceases to give a good goddamn. Which goes to the essentiality of being a pure, unadulterated (but un-adulterous) slut (as opposed to a whore, which is what the publishing industry actually is).

As my post-millennial writing portfolio grew, along with it my desire to get it "out there," I found within my bosom the need for critique, input, feedback.

I hit the literary circuit in earnest. At one conference I found myself, light of $350, in a private session with a "professional" editor, Bohemia Burgmeier, with whom I shared this, my *Second Sluthood,* in its nascent form. She was from some hot-shot la-de-dah New York City big-house publisher, thus the reading fee for the thirty-minute sit-down. She was quite the sarcasmagoric shrew as well, and she would not be tamed.

"First of all, you cannot make reference to the South until halfway in. At the very least a third. Otherwise you've turned off most of the country, especially New York! Hel-*lo?* Where the publishers are?"

She also said, more than once, "Your preposterous prose is ponderously purple."

"I shall wear purple," goes the line from Jenny Joseph's poem on the existence of an elderly renegade. It is only just and fitting that my words be colored as such. Being (shudder) "subtle" is obviously not my modus operandi. Therefore, I spoke directly and to the point: "I find your rabid prejudice against my roots supremely offensive. You are a big city supremacist, that's what you are."

"Oh, puh-lease."

"These bigoted ideas have been programmed into your—"

"I'm following a model that has been proven time and time again."

"Into your vocabulary, into your mind, into your very spirit. If you are a religious woman I would advise you to get down on your knees and beseech the Lord or some-such for forgiveness."

"Have I mentioned that your speech is as purple as the prose?"

"And if *you* were the object of that kind of stereotypical scorn I suppose it would be just fine."

"Once again: Puh-lease. Look. With extensive editing this might have some potential. I mean people might get a—what do you call it?—a 'hoot' out of—"

"God, you sound like Miss Jane Hathaway talking 'hillbilly' to Elly May Clampett."

"—out of this book if you let them get hooked before you say you're from—" she took a deep breath and, with the weight of the Northeast on her shoulders, slowly exhaled, "the *South*."

"But haven't you heard? There *is* no South anymore. We're all the residents of the big blue marble. Universal feelings. Universal attitudes. A glut of belly-flapping, baby-booming, golden-parachute-dragging Americans going global."

"Doesn't matter. They will automatically think this is one of those hokey grits-and-corn pone, you-might-be-a-redneck-if, blue-collar-on-one-end-antebellum-blue-blood-on-the-other stereotypical kinds of things when they get a whiff of your, um, region." She actually wrinkled her nose as if catching the scent of eau d' sour buttermilk.

"Well, I certainly am not 'hokey.' Hokier than *thou,* yes. Hokey, no. And if they automatically assume anything, well that speaks volumes about them as fellow members of the human species. So my attitude is simple: fuck 'em."

"Brilliant strategy. *That* always works."

"Has it ever been tried? Could there be a huge billboard: 'Fuck you. Yours Truly, Ruby Pearl Saffire'? A very simple, direct message, in black and white. Some kind of very sleek and sexy font. You know, very New York, which only adds to the delicious irony."

"Are you insane?"

"Perhaps it is time to think insanely—not merely outside the box, but as if there were *no* box in the first place."

"How do I get you to understand that if it's perceived as regional—"

"But it truly is not regional! Since when did sex and desire and resurrection become regional? Answer: not regional. Damn it to hell."

"Another thing about the manuscript . . . as entertaining as all this is, I just don't see how it's all going to hang together."

"So my thoughts jump a bit."

"A bit? A *bit?* Your thoughts *within* thoughts jump—a bit."

"Ain't it fun?"

"Fun, yes. I just don't know how many readers you will be able to draw in to them—the thoughts. The preponderance of parentheses!"

I gave her my Hannibal Lecter smirk and wink. "*Love* ya alliteration."

"And the italics and the goddamn semi-colons!"

"I'm willing to do a semi-colonostomy. You see? I can compromise."

Sadly, she did not react but continued, "And you want to add self-help to it all? Who are you to offer advice? You're not even a therapist."

"Neither is Dr. Laura, and I make a hell of a lot more sense than she does."

"And have I mentioned that you use the comment, 'I digress' far and away too frequently?"

"This conversation continues to be so alliterative. I do love that."

"And the word 'bosom'!"

"Because it's such a warm, squishy, comforting little word. Look. What wouldst thou have me do?"

"Make a choice. As it is you go from talking about sex to talking about religion and politics. And some of the writing is something like humor. Some is social commentary."

"So? This is one funny, sex-ridden society we live in, don't you think?"

"And then you throw in those crazy poems!" She threw out her arms in a sweeping show of exasperative redundancy.

"I feel certain that professorial types will love my *Roadkill Trilogy*."

A heavy sigh from Ms. Burgmeier.

"And women of a certain age will love my little 'thong' ditty. And if you can't laugh at a few lines about an extricated uterus, well, you don't deserve a sense of humor."

Of course, Ms. B. took grave offense when I confided in her my refusal to fly the friendly skies. "That's it. You'll never get a contract."

"Oh, surely there will be someone out there who can accommodate my trivial little eccentricities."

"*Ever*," she reiterated. "My god, it makes you look like the yokel they will take you to be."

"There are plenty of tres sophisticated, Mensa society folks who fear to fly. I shall research this and report the good company to you."

"That's not the point. These days it goes with the territory."

"What territory?"

"The contract. The *con*tract."

"Oh. That 'con' word. Again, I am not one who is full of respect for the corporate world—even publishing."

"You will be seen as 'difficult.'"

"I care not."

"You're making a huge mistake."

"I cease to give a good goddamn. I will not be a whore."

All true-blue sluts have integrity.

In the end, I felt I had been duped, clipped, taken, flimflammed, "shrewd" by the shrew. Yet the encounter was a valuable object lesson in what has been an ongoing theme of this manifesto and now becomes the aforementioned Tenet Number Eighteen: Thou shalt cease to give a good goddamn.

Continuing on my odyssey in Literary Land, I decided the place to be was in a real creative writing program with a real instructor (as opposed to some big city full-of-herself editor or some impersonal internet site), and plunked down some more serious moolah in order to attend a class at the university. What I expected was guidance, constructive criticism, mentoring, all the warm fuzzies upon which we humans thrive. After all, when one is putting one's deepest musings, often even one's inner tyke, upon the table for all to scrutinize, then one is tres vulnerable.

What I got in this three-hour weekly seminar was a vicious, evil little man determined to chip away at the spirits of the ten students under his tutelage until they were completely broken down (it's a good thing I had ceased to give a good goddamn by then).

Dr. Jaime Prique Blanco (I added the middle name; I have no idea what "prique" means in Spanish; to me it simply means "prick") was of the school of thought that proffered writing programs should be hazings of cruel twists of verbal daggers plunged deep into one's pathetically willing students' hearts. The role of the professor was to be one of ultimate authority, a supreme, all-knowing voice of he who is to be sucked up to, groveled at the feet of, emulated, and feared. Often he would stop a reader after the first paragraph, or even the first sentence, proclaiming the writing "trite," or "hackneyed," or "just plain horrid." On other occasions he might let a student go on and on, all the way to the bitter end, before proclaiming the story to be "language usage of the all-time low variety."

Of course he had a couple of "pets"—both male (he was particularly brutal with the females)—whom he praised from time to time but not enough to make fear a stranger to them. I watched in horror as he reduced his brood, one by one, to mush. Yes, at every turn emotional anguish was prepared to be heaped upon any victim, including yours truly.

"Obviously you aren't serious about writing," was his only lisping comment after my first offering, a bawdy chapter from my novel. I had been observing Satan for three weeks by now and had decided that I was not about to do the dance to which he was accustomed. I was his elder, which is quite a good card to have in one's hand; the others were practically children. I said nothing, but locked my formidable, little-old-lady gaze onto his.

After a few beats he leaned forward, attempting intimidating body language. "Well? What do you have to say?"

I replied in a most pleasant tone, "I was not aware that a question was posed. And I do not care to respond to the rude comments you feel compelled to make."

His face went red. "Then get out. This is a *seminar*. A discussion."

"I am quite aware of what it is. After all, I paid hundreds of dollars in order to have a seat here and I shall not be leaving until I decide to leave. Or perhaps not at all to leave." I gave him my sweetest smile.

"Who do you think—" he sputtered, then, surely perceiving his disadvantage, "Suit yourself."

"Thank you, Mr. Blanco," I replied, as perkily as possible. "I'll do just that."

"*Dr.* Blanco."

"Yes, of course. Do forgive me. I had forgotten."

Yes, I had bested him, and the others knew it, expressing their admiration of my spine outside of class. "You simply have to cease to give a good goddamn," I advised them when queried about my ability to face him down in such a calm and gentle manner. I was unable to contain myself, however, when a darling little girl named Michelle was disemboweled before the group.

She had shared a synopsis of her short story with me, expressing all the insecurity he had fostered within her thus far. It was a compelling tale. She confided that it was inspired by her father's death—very full of those all-powerful inner tyke issues which equates with the opening of one's heart. I truly feared for her.

Lucifer stopped her halfway in. "Is this drivel *going* somewhere? Or is it just you, publicly masturbating?"

She was speechless. Deer. Headlights. The making of tears.

"You are a merciless prick!" It came out before I could check myself.

"I beg your pardon!"

It was too late, of course. The words cascaded from my forked tongue. "You are just the kind of prick who screams to the world, 'Look at *me*. I have this teeny-tiny *prick* so I must compensate with a pathologically *huge* ego that requires the fear and adoration of a bunch of willing young people, who will one day realize what a sham is being perpetrated upon them.'"

"You—you—" he stammered, red-faced, purpling darker.

"Or perhaps you should be saying, 'Look at *me*. I am a self-loathing homosexual has-been who lives in a *humongous* closet and can only sadistically humiliate the young men who look to me for guidance because it gives *me* something to think about whilst masturbating in the shower whilst my beard cooks breakfast. As for the young women, why don't I simply accuse one of *them* of *emotional* masturbation when I am threatened that she might be supremely more talented than I, who have a mere *two* published novels, however many forevers ago, under my belt, the first of which was desperately *self* published.' Yes, Mr. Tightie Whitie, I have done my research."

I looked at Michelle, who was gazing at me, wide-eyed and drop-jawed, as were all of the others save Lucifer, who stood and bellowed, "You! Get! Out!"

I scooped up my notebook. "You're goddamn right I'll get out, but not on *your* orders. I'm leaving because this has been an utter waste of cabbage and I intend to march over to the registrar this very second and demand my money back and I urge everyone else to do the same. I do, however, want to thank you for the opportunity to make a rather dramatic exit, which I do *so* love, you pathetic little, impotent, *impotent* prick!" I then shifted tonal gears. "By the way, Michelle, your story is masterful. Ta-ta, all. *Buenas tardes,* Prique." And I gave the door a mighty slam.

I could go into much detail about Dr. Blanco's preening and fey affectations and boastfulness and plucked eyebrows and inflation of past personal successes, but the little prick deserves no further ink. I had originally planned to include him only as a footnote in this manifesto, but my indignation seized hold of my fingertips.

The silver lining: I am pleased to report that I was successful in getting a goodly portion of my money refunded. As for the other students, I fear they all remained to complete a semester's worth of verbal gutting and dismemberment, for alas, they were young co-eds, with a god-complexed professor to please. I, however, was done with academia in particular and input in general.

Over the course of the next decade, further forays into conferences and such only sealed my conviction that the publishing world was like all other businesses, had even devolved further in the years since my "editing conference" with the Shrew. Long gone were the days of Maxwell Perkins and real relationships between writers and editors, when the agent was not anywhere in the photograph, in the golden era of the first half of the twentieth century, before the arts and athletics were altogether soiled by the love of currency. Alas, I had been birthed much, much too late. Still, I pressed on, friend Opal in tow.

"It seems like we're seeing the same people over and over," Opal said in Memphis. "A lot of the same writers I've never heard of."

"So many books," I said, deflated. "So little time."

"This isn't the RP I know. Not this defeatist. Besides, what if, as you say, they don't ever read your work? Or read it after you are dead and gone? Would you let that change the way you have decided to live your life?"

"Bless you," I said, "for being the slut you are."

For indeed, dear Opal was correct. One should never let the response of others deter one from one's dream. It was a definite insight, although it, like anything worth learning, did not "take" right away. Therefore, I continued to focus on what might be standing in my way, keeping me on the outside looking in on something that was not particularly encouraging. Did I really want to be one of the scores of authors sitting behind rows and rows of tables with stacks of books in front of them, hoping someone might wander up and look at their work, let alone *buy* it? Did I want to be that lone author sitting at a tiny table in a huge bookstore, while nine out of ten people took great pains not to make eye contact lest they have some unwanted book shoved into their unwilling hands?

"Do they always talk so damn much about how hard it is to get published?" Opal asked in Chicago, as my enthusiasm flagged further.

I sighed. "Like winning the lottery."

"Well, girl, you just keep throwing it out there. Somebody's going to come along and give you the right numbers."

"I don't know. It feels dirtier and dirtier all the time. The business, the self-promotion, the sycophants, everything."

Opal sighed. "Yeah. But the saddest part is that so many of these authors nobody's heard of are brilliant. They should be getting attention."

"But they get lost in a sea of pulp and glitz and trash."

"You really feeling the filth?"

I nodded in assertion.

"Then don't do it."

"Quit writing? I could never do that."

"No, fool. Quit doing this."

This, meaning: quit debasing yourself, slinking about these groupings of the famous and wannabe famous, hoping for something like recognition and a shot at publication. It was so like Opal to cut to the chase and lay out the simple truth. And there came upon me a heavenly insight, as the murky slime slid away and crystalline lucidity poured forth into the greening glade of my cragged and tormented mind. I had said it, out loud: "I could never do that," i.e., quit writing. It was not really about getting published, being recognized, etc. It was *absolutely* not about anything as filthy as money. It was simply and exquisitely about my life force. I could not *not* write, no matter what, and Opal had put her beautifully manicured fingernail directly upon it.

I love my friend. I have not gone to a conference or a fest or a symposium since.

⌀

It did not take long for the experience/insight of Ruby P. to spill over into my own relationship with "the business." In fact, the best advice I could give an aspiring writer at this particular and disorienting moment in publishing history is: just do it yourself, by gum—with a couple of very reliable readers who won't lie to you (your mother is out, for example), a damn good editor, and a goddamn good line editor. Pay your editor well and your line editor even better, don't quibble over every little change to make, and do everything else on social media. And this is exactly what Joe and I have decided to do, get shed of those bloodsuckers, Mad Men, and accountants who occupy the no-man's land of middlemen, as our experience with them in general has certainly not been balanced, productive, or equitable. If done wisely, self-publishing need not come off as desperate, as it did in Dr. Jaime Blanco's day. If done wisely, one can beat the middlemen at their own game, without ever engaging with them.

Yes, my husband and I still go to a few conferences—but only to those we truly love and where we want to reunite with the dear friends we've made over the years. The selling of books is secondary. In fact, we'd much rather give away books than fret over the number of sales per quarter. And if a publisher is to be in the mix, we gravitate to the most honorable man we've ever worked with, Joe Taylor at Livingston Press, whose very contracts are written in a comic language that mocks the superficial vein of business that must legally run through our association. It's a satirical language that says, wink-wink, we don't really believe all this shit we're about to sign, because we know it's not about such meaningless clutter. It's the art, stupid.

Which brings me back around to Cris Mazza's delightfully middle-fingered question: "What does one 'win' in art?" A better contract? A big advance? A growing fan base? Am I impractical and naïve to scorn the greed that is baked in to most business ventures? When I take pride in the fact that I suck at capitalism do I worry about alienating potential investors? What if I never get picked up by a big publishing house?

It seems to me that there is only one good answer to those questions, and I have Miss Ruby to thank for that:

I have ceased to give a good goddamn.
Process *that*.

Dirt, Death, and the Divine: The Roots of Southern Writing

River Jordan

ew things focus a southerner down to the essence of what it means to be southern more than someone from other backgrounds, ethnicities, countries, or other parts asking us questions. Nowhere are we more southern than when we venture out beyond the borders of sweet tea.

When questions are posed to me from those who are either confused or enamored with all things southern, and, if anyone can break it down for them, then give way the stage to my tribe—the southern writer.

One of the great pleasures of my life has been to be included and counted among the alumni of the Kindlings, a type of Tolkiens movement in the United States. The one fashioned after Tolkien and C. S. Lewis sitting in the pub drinking, smoking pipes, and discussing God and the power of story. A few years ago I was at the Kindlingsfest at Orcas Island, Washington, sitting around a table of alumni where bottles of old scotch graced the table along with the deep faith and intelligence, conversation and camaraderie. Someone asked me one afternoon around that table on Dick Staub's front porch, what makes a southern writer different from any other? While I couldn't answer for everyone or even from a standpoint of academic correction, I could only answer from personal experience. Well, for me when I read a writer from say New York I think, oh, they are so smart. I could swear I actually hear their brain ticking. But when I read a southern writer I can feel their heart beating. That's how I know it's southern. By the heartbeat.

If that had been a test, I passed with flying colors.

My dear old mother-in-law who was so near to my heart was what I considered a surenuff Yankee because of her mindset and her experience.

Well, that and she was from the North. She would constantly question me, "But why do you . . ." fill in the southern question of the week. Or she would say, "God, you southerners!" Like the time my sister brought Daddy's ashes to Christmas Dinner. The kind of behavior that perplexed her and was second nature to me. I'm sure she'd laugh at the fact that years after her death, when I was getting divorced from her son, I rocked with her ashes and cried and talked to her. Which by the way I realized the next day when I was with a friend and mentioned this, and by the look on her face this was not everyday fare for your everyday person. What do you expect? I asked her. I come by my southern gothic honest.

⌀

Oh us southerners, bless our dear sweet hearts. The Earth itself breathes us into being. Dirt, death, and divinity. These are the things that we are born believing in. We can try to shake it, deny it, run from it. But our believing it's as true as our blood coursing through our veins.

In the beginning . . . that's the first line of the big story. It's the *listen close because it's coming*. Southerners draw from a well that is a mystical blend of raw earth and our peopled history. From the storytellers that bore us because all those that came before us were storytellers. And, yes, the dirt. It always comes back to the dirt.

Not in a Tara, *Gone with the Wind* kind of way. I was never a fan of Scarlett.

Hush your mouth!

I can't relate. Don't know no Scarlett.

My people were cotton pickers. Sharecroppers. Poor and hungry. Scarlett just makes me mad. Spoiled rotten. She has to break down and make a dress out of curtains. She gets hungry—finally. Maybe I was just too young when I saw this to appreciate it. Maybe I should finally give up and read the book. Maybe Scarlett is spoiled and doesn't represent the South I know and therefore makes me a little nervous that because of the huge success of the book and the movie, most people will think this is the true South. A place of plantations and privilege. What I know is a different truth. It's real, raw, and reckless.

It's that truth that has infused my writing. A touch of lightning here. A dose of premonition there. The fact of Jesus everywhere.

I could no more pretend to be a different kind of writer than step out the door and speak fluent French. The experience of this backwoods childhood is the memory that I bring to every page. What we bring to the page is our truth. When we do that, what we say is universal and the writer angels smile.

Writers of the southern variety will stop in the midst of everything to watch storm clouds roll in something fierce. To feel the wind blow like there shall be no tomorrow. To watch sunlight glint on the wing of a dragonfly. We will infuse our work with something that lives beyond the borders of this timed existence. To brush the hem of that thing that is out there calling always—the eternal mystery. We are fluent in the mystery of earth meets man, entices, romances, and devours him. Of soul-longing and satisfaction.

It's right there in those fresh biscuits, in the sugared sweetness of that tea, the rhythmic sound of the shelling of the peas. There is that bittersweet taste of all that is good for just this moment as the whisper of death lingers near. We know. That this life is for a time, a short season and it's gone. We funeralize, we open casket, we sing, lament, and journey on, telling stories of what had been. Who has been.

There are other blends of southern. There is cute. My people were not cute. There is well to do, genteel, soft, and surface smooth polite. Those aren't my people either. My people wore no pedigrees. Earned no degrees. Were tough as nails.

Those days and nights we hung on the porch may be cliché in this modern tech society. But the porch was the backbone of our storytelling. The way Uncle Edie Lewis would lean in to tell a story. Or tell James Earl to tell one of his. A particular story over and over again. To the same listeners year in and year out. Relatives dear and dead. Cliché by now maybe but the truth is—porch happens. When the porches all finally disappear, when the back-yard steps are replaced with the kind of yards manicured to perfection, then the days of real southern writers will shift and slip away. Assimilation will be complete and southern will be no more. But I think that time is still a virtual reality away.

One particular night plays over and over again in my memory of being a child. Fourish I was. Sleeping with my Grandmother and her long, lean back turned to the wall before me. Me awake when all other children would be asleep. An insomniac even at that age, the last to find the way into dream. The windows were open as always in the summertime. It was the way we lived. We prayed for a breeze, for rain, for a break from the heat. But on this night there was heat lightning that stretched out across the sky, that moved toward the house, that rolled in the distance, drew near. This power. This unescapable unleashed flash. This show. I watched in a hushed awe, mesmerized and unafraid. A great power had come upon but not consumed me. I alone to witness. The safety of my Grandmother's hushed breath. My trust of her. My knowing that what approached was untamable. Unnamable. And, that to that power I belonged.

We came from the earth. Dirt beneath our druthers. Spit and venom, a whip of intention unleashed on page and pronoun. Turn the page of any story where southern meets you and there you feel it, the unmistakable heartbeat that will not be denied.

What spins beneath us remains no mystery but courses through our veins. The earth beats and we feel it. The earth bleeds and we mourn it. Seed falls on good ground and we reap a harvest of words. The earth throws lightning and we catch it.

Sky splitting. Us children, small, huddled on a porch. Hushed excitement as Uncle John points, whispers, "Watch," and in that whisper all amens. This was sight beholden. Who could doubt God with such power manifest? Who else could capture this rare token of the wild? Our attention electrified. Our watching baptizing us. We are born again in imaginations. Soul sister, soul brother. Electrified by night. The rain forthcoming. The thunder rolling, banging hard against the heavens. Who in their right mind would not believe in dirt and death and the divine one this night? We are caught betwixt all things. The smell of sky and dirt colliding just before the rain. The sound of drops hitting on the tin roof as we were huddled inside to dry. Hurried to open windows where Granny pulled us back, rushed to close the window. Us sleeping then, the ground full wet as seeds awakened. The corn we would be shucking soon sucking up the wet. The peas for shelling turning green inside their beds. All things moving on toward completion, fulfilling season upon season, sweeping us into years, into one big story marching ever onward into the great hereafter.

Memaw never went to church. Didn't have to. She was good down to the core and her believing came up natural. Nothing in her was lost to God. She sowed and she reaped. She cooked in a kitchen that sweltered in the summer. Threw off heat like a coal furnace. A little gas stove, baking, cooking three a day. In the summer her standing there, her face wet, her apron tied, the fan on high. Lord, have mercy. What strange, strong stock we come from. The kitchen cooling as the burners quit and we were called to dinner. Cousins all, Grandad, aunts and uncles. The food was loaves and fishes. The table held more people than it could. We cozied up so distracted by the bounty that we forgot the lack of distance between elbows, thighs, and knees.

Silence—never. Ever. Not once do I remember a meal, a porch, a yard, a boat, that didn't offer stories there. Not once an awkward silence, stone cold shoulder, frozen stare. In all there flowed stories told by one, heard by all. A rolling thunder of a laugh that followed, echoed through the little house. All the little houses. Tiny places that filled a multitude with no pause or apology.

There is this. The truth and nothing but the truth. Southerners who are true to the bone are born and bred by three solid things—dirt, death, and the divine. All things come from these. The dirt that claims us at birth in righteous and unknowing ways. Always certain that once we are born to the South we will not escape it. Not inside. A woman at the Nashville's Day of the Dead Tequila Festival struck up a conversation with me. She was from Brooklyn but had moved to Tennessee years ago and entered into a two-year relationship with her boyfriend, but she confided he had just broken up with her. When she'd asked him why, he'd explained it was because she wasn't southern. Then she asked me if that was the truth as if I'd know. I did. I thought about it. She was very New York. All in New York. If I'd guessed I would have said she was a Mets fan but would cheer for the Yankees over Boston. "Yes," I told her. "It was. For him anyway."

"But, why?" It was a lament for understanding. "The Civil War was years ago. It's over." Tequila can bring on lamenting and telling strangers your sad everythings.

"It's not about the Civil War," I tried to explain. Tequila can bring on explaining. "It's about the dirt."

"Dirt?"

"Yes, we are attached to the dirt. The actual, physical, geological mud, swamp, river, rock, dirt. We near 'bout eat it. If a good southerner moved to another country and became a beautiful ex-pat living the life on some dis-quieted happy foreign soil and some friend showed up from the deep South and produced a jar with dirt from 'back home,' that person would open that jar and take a deep breath, pour some in her hand, clutch it and cry. That's what happens."

"That's crazy."

"That's southern, baby."

"That's another thing. All that generic southern name calling."

"What, the 'baby'? You would prefer honey? Sugar?"

"I would prefer my boyfriend not leave me for the South."

"It's not so easily defined. If you hooked up with the kinda southern boy I imagine, he had spent his summers running half wild in the country, hanging out on porches, down by creeks, under bridges. Turned about fourteen and started driving somebody's old pickup around on those back country roads. He take you riding in a pickup?"

"To do what?"

"Umm, there's your problem. Riding around in a pickup is the doing. Don't need anything else. Pickup truck and some dirt. Add a little Southern Comfort and some moonlight to that and you got yourself a top-notch date there, darlin'."

I like this girl. I want to teach her to eat boiled peanuts with the window down, to listen to Merle Haggard and skip stones in a creek. To howl at the moon and go skinny dipping. I want to teach her how to be a southern girl and get that man back she loved for so long.

"Then there is God."

"If we going to talk God, honey, we are gonna need another taste."

This is easy as we are approaching the front of the line for a sample of Blue Agave.

"I believe in God. Well, I don't not believe in God. You know what I'm saying? I mean it's there but it's not something that needs to be out on the table all the time. Right? Am I right? I mean you're drinking tequila. You don't seem religious. You get it."

"Did your boyfriend drink tequila?"

"He did."

"It's not tequila or the lack thereof. God in the South wears a face and the face is Jesus. And Jesus to a southerner is as real as mud and biscuits."

"What do you mean?"

I sip a slow burn and try to get my words to come out right. "You ever see one of those pictures of Jesus where his eyes seem to follow you all over the room?"

"No."

"Well, it doesn't matter. That's the way southerners feel about Jesus. He is eyeing you all the time. Which means he expects certain things out of you. To say grace at Easter, to respect your Mama, and to remember your people that have passed on—God rest their souls."

"Dead people?"

"A dearly departed, crossed over, cloud of witnesses kind of dead. Which, in spite of the fact that we will see them in the sweet by and by, we keep them propped up on this side telling stories."

"About them? The dead people?"

"Not so much." Someone pushes me in the crowd and since I am talking about Jesus I refrain from pushing them back. "We tell the stories they told."

"About . . ."

"People that died before them." We toss our little glasses in the trash.

"So, it's not about the war."

"We don't remember the war," I tell her. "It's more organic than that."

"But he called me a Yankee."

"There are worse things to be called. It's just his way of saying you came from different dirt."

We got in three more lines. I asked her about New York and Nashville and how she got down here in the first place. Then I went one way and she went the other.

The deep South for a writer is all those things. That collective memory of our people. Those nights of moonlight and pickup trucks. Summers full of mud and laughter on a creek. A grandmother in the kitchen. Jesus fans, family Bibles. Funerals and fun times. Separating one from the other isn't just not probable, it's not possible.

Combined, these beautiful elements make up the perfect recipe for the kind of writing that creates reader fans across the globe. Cut us and we bleed story. We are the very fabric of story with an unmistakable texture and substance that is solely southern. It is all things that sign—Southern by the Grace of God—declares.

A Life in Books
From *Dimestore: A Writer's Life*

Lee Smith

J was a reader long before I was a writer. In fact, I started writing in the first place because I couldn't stand for my favorite books to be over, so I started adding more and more chapters onto the ends of them, often including myself as a character. Thus the Bobbsey twins became the Bobbsey triplets, and Nancy Drew's best friends, Bess Marving and George Fayne, were joined by another character named Lee Smith—who actually ended up with Ned Nickerson! The additional chapters grew longer and more complicated as my favorite books became more complicated—*Heidi*, *Anne of Green Gables*, and *Pippi Longstocking*, for instance.

Mama was indefatigable in reading aloud to me when I was little, and I'm sure that the musical cadence of her soft southern voice is one reason I took to reading the way I did, for the activity itself was so pleasurable. Later, we pored over the huge pages of the *National Enquirer* together, marveling at the lives of the stars, the psychic who could bend spoons with the power of his mind alone, and that Indiana couple who got kidnapped and taken away in a space ship where they were given physical examinations by aliens before being dropped back down into their own cornfield, none the worse for wear. Mama and I loved this stuff. My father read a lot of newspapers, magazines, and sometimes history or politics. Though neither of my parents read novels, they received the *Reader's Digest* Condensed Books, which I devoured, and they also encouraged me to go to our fledgling library.

This soon got out of hand. I became a voracious, then an obsessive reader; recurrent bouts of pneumonia and tonsillitis gave me plenty of time to indulge my passion. After I was pronounced "sickly," I got to stay home a lot, slathered with a vile salve named Mentholatum, spirit lamp hissing in the corner of my room, reading to my heart's content. I remained an inveterate reader of the sort who hides underneath the covers with a flashlight and reads all night long. But I did not read casually, or for mere information. What I wanted was to feel all wild and trembly inside, an effect first produced by *The Secret Garden*, which I'd read maybe twenty times.

The only man I had ever loved as much as Colin of *The Secret Garden* was Johnny Tremain, from Esther Forest's book of that title. I used to wish it was *me*—not Johnny Tremain—who'd had the hot silver spilled on my hand. I would have suffered anything (everything!) for Johnny Tremain.

Other books had affected me strongly: *Little Women*, especially the part where Beth dies, and *Gone With the Wind*, especially the part where Melanie dies. I had long hoped for a wasting disease, such as leukemia, to test my mettle. I also loved *Marjorie Morningstar*, *A Tree Grows in Brooklyn*, and books like *Dear and Glorious Physician*, *The Shoes of the Fisherman*, *Christy*, and anything at all about horses and saints. I had read all the Black Stallion books, of course, as well as all the Marguerite Henry books. But my all-time favorite was a book about Joan of Arc, especially the frontispiece illustration depicting Joan as she knelt and "prayed without ceasing for guidance from God," whose face was depicted overhead in a thunderstorm. Not only did I love Joan of Arc, I wanted to *be* her.

I was crazy for horses and saints.

"By the way," my mother mentioned to me one day almost casually while I was home being sick in bed and she was straightening my covers, "You know, Marguerite Henry stayed at your grandmother's boarding house on Chincoteague Island while she was writing that book."

"What book?" I sat right up.

"*Misty*," Mama said. "Then she came back to write *Sea Star*, and I think the illustrator, Wesley Dennis, stayed there, too. Cousin Jack used to take him out on a boat."

I couldn't believe it! A real writer, a horse writer, had walked up the crushed oyster shell road where I had gone barefoot, had sat at the big dinner table where I'd eaten fish and corncakes for breakfast; had maybe even swung in the same wicker porch swing I loved.

I wrote a novel on the spot, on eight sheets of my mother's Crane stationery. It featured as main characters my two favorite people at that time: Adlai Stevenson and Jane Russell. In my novel, they fell in love and then went West together in a covered wagon. Once there they got married and became—inexplicably!—Mormons. I am not sure how I knew about Mormons. But even at that age, I was fixed upon romance, flight, and religion, themes I would return to again and again.

What did my parents think of this strange little girl who had come to them so late in life, after they had become resigned to never having children? Well, they spoiled me rotten and were simply delighted by everything I did, everything I showed any interest in. I believe if I told my mother that I wanted to be, say, an ax murderer, she would have said, without blinking an eye, "Well, that's nice dear, what do you think you might want to major in?" My daddy would have gone out to buy me the ax.

Though my parents might feel—as Mama certainly said later—that they wished I would just stop all that writing stuff and marry a lawyer or a doctor, which is what a daughter really ought to do, of course, the fact is that they were so loving that they gave me the confidence, and the permission, early on, to do just about anything I wanted to do. Decades later, I would realize how unusual this was, and how privileged I have been because of it. Now I see this issue—permission to write—as the key issue for many women I have worked with in my classes, especially women who have begun writing later in their lives.

But my childhood was not entirely a happy one. No writer's childhood ever is. There was my father's inexplicable sadness and my mother's "nerves"; there was my strange Uncle Tick; there was a scary little neighborhood "club" we formed, which did bad things. There was a lot of drinking. There were hospitalizations and long absences and periods of being sent away to live with other relatives. Life was often confusing and mysterious, which inspired Martha Sue and my cousin Randy and me to start our own espionage firm, which I would describe much later in a short story named "Tongues of Fire":

We lived to spy, and this is mainly what we did on our bike trips around town. We'd seen some really neat stuff, too. For instance we had seen Roger Ainsley, the coolest guy in our school, squeezing pimples in his bathroom mirror. We had seen Mister Bondurant whip son Earl with a belt, and later, when Earl suddenly dropped out of school and enlisted in the Army, we alone knew why. We had seen our fourth-grade teacher, prissy Miss Emily Horn, necking on a couch with her boyfriend, and smoking cigarettes. Best of all, we had seen Mrs. Cecil Hertz come running past a picture window wearing nothing but an apron, followed shortly by Mr. Cecil Hertz himself, wearing nothing at all and carrying a spatula.

It was amazing how careless people were about drawing their drapes and pulling their shades down. It was amazing what you could see, especially if you were an athletic and enterprising girl such as myself. I wrote my observations down in a Davy Crockett spiral notebook I'd bought for this purpose. I wrote down everything: date, time, weather, physical descriptions, my reaction. I would use all this stuff later, in my novels.

This is true. And though it's also true that we actually did spy on people, that first paragraph is mostly made up. When you write fiction, you up the ante, generally speaking, since real life rarely affords enough excitement or conflict to spice up a page sufficiently. This passage also illustrates another technique that has saved my neck—maybe even my life—many times: the use of humor to allow us to talk or write about the scariest things, things we couldn't articulate and deal with otherwise. It is another way of whistling past the graveyard.

⌁

My first actual novel was named *The Last Day the Dogbushes Bloomed* (1969), and its main character was a weird little nine-year-old girl named Susan, much like this very same nine-year-old girl we have been talking about. She was often a solitary child, though her imaginary friends and pursuits were legion. In this excerpt, she describes her favorite hideout, her "wading house."

The way to the wading house was hard. That's what was so good about it. After I got there, no scouts could track me down. First I went out from under the other side of the dogbushes, then I went by a secret path through the blackberry bushes, which tried to grab me as I went by. They reached out their hands at me but I got away. When I came to the riverbank, I walked on the rocks to the wading house. That way, if anybody chased me with dogs, they would lose the trail.

The wading house was not a real house. It was a soft, light green tree, a willow that grew by the bank. The way the branches came down, they made a little house inside them. The land and the tiny river were both inside the house, and it was the only wading house in the world, and I was the only one that knew about it. It was a very special place.

There were a lot of other people that lived there too and they were my good friends. There was a young lizard named Jerry, because I didn't know if it was a boy or a girl, and Jerrys can go either way. Jerry had a long, shiny tail and he stayed mostly in the weeds but he would come out to say hello to me every time I came. A very wise old grandfather turtle lived there too. He blinked his eyes slow at me, and I could tell that he knew everything there was to know. Grandfather Turtle had three silly daughters, but I liked them because they were so cute. Their shells were like the rug in the Trivettes' living room, brown and green by turns. The big rock by the side of the river was not a rock at all, it was a secret apartment house. A baby blacksnake sat on the top. He was so black and fast that it hurt you to look at him. On the second floor, the sides of the rock, there lived a family of little brown bugs. They were also busy and never had much time to play. The worms did, though. They lived on the ground floor under the rock, and I liked them almost best of all. I never knew a family that had so much fun. All they ever did was wiggle and laugh.

After I said hi to everybody in the wading house I liked to sit under the big tree on the bank and think about a lot of things. There were a lot of things to think about then, and there was nothing to keep from thinking about like there is now. Or sometimes I would sit, like that day, and look at everything very hard so it would stay in my head for always.

What this little narrator is trying very hard not to think about is that her family is breaking up because the mother has run off with a man. This was an entirely fictional plot of course, but a novel must have conflict; conflict is the single absolutely necessary ingredient of fiction.

As soon as my book was accepted, I was really excited, of course, and sent a copy to my parents. I waited anxiously for their reply, but I heard nothing. Finally I called them up on the "long-distance telephone," as we used to say then.

My mother answered.

"Have you read my book?" I asked.

"Yes, I have," she said.

"Well, how did you like it?" I asked.

"Not much," my mother said. "In fact, I have thrown it in the river."

"*What?*" I said. "What's wrong with it?"

"Everybody in this town is going to think I ran off with a man," my mother said.

"Mama, that's just crazy," I said. "Look, you're still there. You and daddy have been married for thirty years."

"It doesn't matter," my mother said. "That's what they'll think anyway. So I am taking steps to make sure that they are not going to read it, any of them."

"Wait a minute," I said. "What steps?"

"I have told your father that he cannot order the book," she said—my father's Ben Franklin dimestore being naturally the only place in town where you could possibly buy a book—"And I have told Lillian Elgin that she cannot order the book either." Mama's friend, Lillian Elgin, was the town librarian.

So, that was it! Total censorship! Nobody in town ever read that first book, or the second book either. My mother banned that one because it had sex in it. But that was just as well, I guess, because it was also just awful, as second novels sometimes are if we write them too soon, having used up our entire life so far, all the great traumas and dramas of our youth, in the first one. My second was all about a sensitive English major who keeps having disastrous yet generic romances; luckily, publishing it was exactly like throwing it in the river.

❦

But now I was in big trouble, as a writer. I had used up my childhood. I had used up my adolescence, and I had nothing more to say. I had used up my whole life! Furthermore I was happily married to the poet James Seay, my first husband, so there was also no conflict, that necessary cauldron of creativity.

But luckily, by then I was a reporter working at The *Tuscaloosa News* in Tuscaloosa, Alabama, where my editor assigned me to cover the all-south majorette contest taking place on the campus of the University of Alabama. This was an enormous contest with categories you might expect—such as "Fire Baton" and "Best Personality"—but also a lot of categories you might not expect, such as "Improvisation to a Previously Unheard Tune," which I thought was a riot. The winner of the whole thing would be called Miss Fancy Strut. The girls were really sweet, because they were all trying to get Miss Personality, which would give them a lot of extra points, but their mothers were just bitches from hell, very competitive. Anyway, it lasted for days, and then finally all the points from all the categories were tallied up, and the winner turned out to be a beautiful little blonde girl from Opp, Alabama, whom I had to interview.

So I asked, of course, "How does it feel to be Miss Fancy Strut?"

And she said, with tears streaming down her face, "This is the happiest moment of my life!"

I was completely stunned, because I could tell this was true, and I was thinking, Oh honey it's going to be a long downhill slide from here. You are so young to peak out like this.

You will not be surprised to learn that my next novel was named *Fancy Strut*, and it was all about majorettes and their mamas. It was a real breakthrough for me, because nobody in it was anything like me at all. Finally I had made that necessary imaginative leap—which is a real necessity, since most of us writers can't be out there living like crazy all the time. These days, very few are the writers whose book jackets list things like bush pilot, big game hunter, or exotic dancer.

No, more often we are English teachers. We have children, we have mortgages, we have bills to pay. So we have to stop writing strictly about what we know, which is what they always told us to do in creative writing classes. Instead we have to write about what we can learn, and what we can imagine, and thus we come to experience that great pleasure Anne Tyler noted when somebody asked her why she writes, and she answered, "I write because I want more than one life." Let me repeat that: "I write because I want more than one life."

And let me tell you, this is the greatest privilege, and the greatest pleasure, in the world. Over the years I have moved away from autobiography to write about housewives and whores, serpent handlers and beauticians, country music singers and evangelists and nineteenth-century schoolteachers—lots of people I will never be, living in times and places I have never been. But somewhere along the way, I have also come to realize that the correspondences between real life and fiction are infinitely more complicated than I would have ever guessed as a younger woman.

Peter Taylor once said, "I write in order to find out what I think." This is certainly true for me, too, and often I don't even know what I think until I go back and read what I've written. My belief is that we have only one life, that this is all there is. And I refuse to lead an unexamined life. No matter how painful it may be, I want to know what's going on. So I write fiction the way other people write in their journals.

My husband, Hal, has been heard to bemoan my lack of self-knowledge. He envisions our respective psyches like this: his is a big room in a factory, brightly lit. He's got uniformed guys in there carrying clipboards and constantly working on all his problems, checking gauges and levels, in day and night shifts. He's always monitoring their work, reading their reports. He sees my mind, by contrast, as a dark forest with no path, where huge beasts loom up at you suddenly out of the night and then disappear, only to return again and again.

Maybe so. But when I read what I've written, I know what they are.

In 1980, for instance, I wrote a novel named *Black Mountain Breakdown*, about a girl named Crystal Spangler who is so busy fitting herself into others' images of her (first fulfilling her mother's beauty-queen dreams, then altering her image to please the various men in her life) that she loses her own true self and finally ends up paralyzed: "Crystal just lies up there in that room every day, with her bed turned cattycorner so she could look out the window and see Lorene's climbing rambler rose in full bloom on the trellis if she would turn her head. But she won't. She won't lift a finger. She just lies there. Everybody in town takes a fancy to it" . . . feeding her jello, brushing her hair, reading *The Reader's Digest* out loud to her. The most terrifying aspect of her condition is that "Crystal is happy . . . as outside her window the seasons come and go and the colors change on the mountain." When I wrote that, my first marriage should have ended years earlier, something I'd been unable to face or even admit; later, reading those words over, I finally understood how I'd felt during the last part of that marriage. I was able then to deal with its inevitable ending, and move on with my life.

No matter what I may think I am writing about at any given time—majorettes in Alabama, or a gruesome, long-ago murder, or the history of country music—I have come to realize that it is all, finally, about me, often in some complicated way I won't come to understand until years later. But then it will be there for me to read, and I will understand it, and even if I don't know who I am now, I will surely have a record of who I was then.

⌥

Writing is also my addiction, for the moment when I am writing fiction is that moment when I am most intensely alive. This "aliveness" does not seem to be mental, or not exactly. I am certainly not thinking while I write. Whatever I'm doing is almost the opposite of thinking. Especially during the pre-writing phase, when I am simply making up the story and imagining its characters, and during those first drafts, I feel a dangerous, exhilarating sense that anything can happen.

It reminds me of a woman in eastern Kentucky I interviewed years ago when I was writing about serpent-handling believers. I had seen her lift a double handful of copperheads high in the air during a religious service. Now we faced each other across a little Formica table in a fast-food restaurant, drinking Cokes and eating fries. I asked the obvious: "Why do you do this, when it's so dangerous? You could die any time." She merely smiled at me, a beautiful, generous smile without a trace of irony.

"Honey," she began, "I do it out of an intense desire for holiness." She smiled at me again, while that sank in. "And I'll tell you something else, too. When you've held the serpent in your hands, the whole world kind of takes on an edge for you."

I could see that. Chill bumps arose on my arms as she spoke. For I was once the girl who had embarrassed her mother so much by rededicating my life over and over at various revivals, coming home dripping wet from total immersion in those standup pools from Sears that they set up in the little tents behind the big revival tents, or simply in the fast-flowing creeks that rushed down the mountainsides.

And the feeling I get when I'm writing intensely is much the same.

For me, writing is a physical joy. It is almost sexual—not the moment of fulfillment, but the moment when you open the door to the room where your lover is waiting, and everything else falls away.

It does fall away, too. For the time of the writing, I am nobody. Nobody at all. I am a conduit, nothing but a way for the story to come to the page. Oh, but I am terribly alive then, too, though I say I am no one at all; my every sense is keen and quivering. I can smell the bacon cooking downstairs in my grandmother's kitchen that winter morning in 1952, I can feel the flowered carpet under my bare feet as I run down the hall, I can see the bright blue squares of the kitchen wallpaper, bunches of cherries alternating with little floral bouquets. Sun shines through the frost on the windowpanes, almost blinding me; my granddaddy's Lucky Strike cigarette smoke still hangs in the air, lazy blue, though he is already up and gone he had walked the bridge across the river to the old stone courthouse where he will work all day long as the county treasurer. I love my granddaddy, who always wears a hat and a dark blue suit. I do not love my grandmother so much, who tells me not to be a tomboy and keeps moistening her lips with her tongue in a way I hate. I wish my mother would get out of the hospital so I could go home. I don't see why I can't stay with Daddy, anyway. I could make us peanut butter sandwiches for dinner, and cut the crusts off.

See what I mean? I am there now, and I want to stay there. I hate to leave that kitchen and come back to this essay.

All my senses are involved when I am writing fiction, but it is hearing that is most acute. This has always been true. I can see everything in the story, of course—I have to see that kitchen in order to walk through it; the icy river, in order to get my grandfather across the bridge. I make a lot of maps before I start writing. Scotch-taping them to the wall. But I am not a visual person in real life. I never know how high to hang pictures, for instance, or where the furniture should go. None of my clothes match. It was words I loved first, words and sentences and music and stories, the voice that comes out of the dark when you're almost asleep, sitting in somebody's lap on a porch, trying to keep your eyes open long enough to hear the end of the story.

So a story always comes to me in a human voice, speaking not exactly into my ear but somewhere deep inside me. If I am writing from a first-person point of view, it is always the voice of the person who is telling the story. If I am writing from a third-person point of view, it is simply the voice of the story itself. Sometimes this voice is slow and pondering, or tentative and unsure. Sometimes it is flat and reportorial; just the facts, ma'am. Sometimes it's gossipy, intimate—a tale told over a Coke and a cigarette during a work break at Food City. Sometimes it's sad, a long, wailing lament, telling and retelling again and again how he done me wrong. It can be furious or vengeful: "I hated him from the moment I first laid eyes on him, hated him instinctively, as if I knew somehow what he would do to our family . . ." It can be a reliable narrator—or an unreliable narrator, sometimes even more interesting. It can be a meditative, authoritative voice, told as if from the distant past or from a great and somehow definitive distance (I confess that ever since we moved into this old house where I work in an upstairs office looking out over the town, this has happened more frequently!).

The most thrilling, of course, is when it is a first-person voice telling a story of real urgency. At these times, all I have to do is keep up; I become a stenographer, a court secretary, a tape recorder. My biggest job is making sure that I have several uninterrupted hours whenever I sit down to write, so this can happen. Whenever a story like this is in process, it is so exciting that I will do almost anything to get those hours—break appointments, call in sick, tell lies. I become a person on drugs. Somebody in the throes of a passionate affair. I'll do anything to get there, to make it happen again. I know I can't ignore the voice, or waste it. I may be a fool, but I'm not that kind of a fool.

Since the writing of fiction is such a physical and personal process for me, I have to write in longhand, still. I have to write with a pen or pencil on a legal pad. I can't have anything mechanical between my body and the page. Later, I'll type it on a computer in order to revise. I can compose nonfiction directly on the computer, but not fiction. Perhaps it's because fiction is so messy, like life. Often I jot down three or four words before I hit upon the right one—or I hope it's the right one. So I mark all the others out, and go on writing, but I want to keep them all, all those words I thought about first and then discarded. I also want to keep that paragraph of description I marked out, and that earlier section about how Ray drowned the dog when he was eleven, and that chapter form the point of view of the mother, because I might change my mind later on and include them. The novel, at this point, is organic, living, changing; anything can still happen, and probably will. This is true up until the very moment when I print the whole thing out and put it into its little coffin, usually an old paper box. Then I hit that SEND button and it's gone to the publisher. Then it's dead, they're all dead, all those people who have been my familiars, who have lived under my skin for weeks and month or years, and I am no longer a writer, but a murderer and mourner, infinitely more alone in the world.

⌖

Writing can also give us the chance to express what is present but mute, or unvoiced, in our own personalities . . . because we are all much more complicated and various people than our lives allow.

During the early eighties, the mountains where I came from began to change rapidly. The fast food restaurants were in around the bend of the Levisa River near my parents' house, for instance, and those satellite TV dishes sprouted like weird mushrooms on every hillside—meaning that the children growing up there wouldn't sound like I do, or like their grandmothers did, but like Walter Cronkite instead. That's when I began to tape my relatives and elderly mountain friends, collecting the old stories, songs, and histories in earnest, with the aim of preserving the type of speech—Appalachian English—and the ways of life of a bygone era. But then a very strange thing happened to me. In *Oral History*, the first novel I wrote using this material exclusively, a voice began speaking who was truly me, in a way in which all these other, more contemporary, and ostensibly autobiographical characters were not—although she (Granny Younger, an old mountain midwife) was certainly more removed from me in time, and place, and circumstance, than any other character I'd ever come up with.

Here is what she says in the first chapter of my novel *Oral History*:

> . . . I'll tell it all directly.
>
> I'll tell it all, but don't you forget it is Almarine's story. Almarine's, and Pricey Jane's, and Lord yes, it's that red-headed Emmy's. Mought be it's her story moren the rest. Iffen twas my story, I never would tell it at all. There's tales I'll tell, and tales I won't. And iffen twas my story, why I'd be all hemmed in by the facts of it like Hoot Owl Holler is hemmed in by them three mountains. I couldn't move no way but forward. And often in my traveling over these hills I have seed that what you want the most, you find offen the beaten path. I never find nothing I need on the trace, for an instance. I never find ary a thing. But I am an old, old woman, and I have traveled a lot in these parts. I have seed folks come and I have seed them go. I have cotched more babies than I can name you; I have put the burying quilts around many a soul. I said I know moren you know and mought be I'll tell you moren you want to hear. I'll tell you a story that's truer than true, and nothing so true is so pretty. It's blood on the moon, as I said. The way I tell a story is the way I want to, and iffen you mislike it, you don't have to hear.

Granny Younger is expressing that part of me that is the writer part, that knows things I don't know, and that does not find its expression in another role I perform—as mother, wife, or teacher for instance.

Writing has become a source of strength for me, too. I had barely begun a novel named *Fair and Tender Ladies*—intended as an honest account and a justification, really, of the lives of so many resourceful mountain women I'd grown up among, women whose plain and home-centered lives are not much valued in the world at large—when my beloved mother went into her last illness, a long and drawn-out sequence of falls, emphysema, and finally heart failure. This period coincided with the onset of Josh's schizophrenia; I spent two years visiting hospitals, sitting by hospital beds, often reading students' work as I tried to hold on to my teaching job. I don't know what

I would have done if I hadn't been writing that novel. I worked on it a bit every day; it was like an open door to another world, another place for me to be for a little while.

Its heroine, Ivy Rowe, grew stronger and stronger, the more I needed her. Every terrible thing in the world happened to her—extreme poverty, too many children, heartbreak, illness, the death of a child—but she could take it. She hung in there, so I did, too. Ivy made sense of her life through writing a constant stream of letters: to her children, to her friends, to her sisters—especially to her favorite sister, Silvaney, even though Silvaney had died young and would never read most of them. Near the novel's end, Ivy burns all her letters, and it is finally my own voice as well as hers that concludes:

> . . . The smoke from the burning letters rose and was lost in the clouds.
> . . . With every one I burned, my soul grew lighter, lighter, as if it rose too with the smoke. And I was not even cold, long as I'd been out there. For I came to understand something in that moment . . . which I had never understood in all these years.
> The letters didn't mean anything.
> Not to the dead girl Silvaney, of course—*nor to me.*
> Nor had they ever.
> It was the *writing* of them, that signified.

In 2003 I had done a lot of historical research but had barely begun a novel named *On Agate Hill* when Josh died. My grief—and rage—were indescribable: "oceanic," to use one doctor's terminology. He told me that there are basically two physiological reactions to grief. Some people sleep a lot, gain weight, become depressed and lethargic.

I had the other reaction—I felt like I was standing with my finger stuck in an electric outlet, all the time. I couldn't sleep. I couldn't read. I couldn't eat. I couldn't remember anything, anything at all. I forgot how to drive to the grocery store. I couldn't find the school where I had taught for twenty years. In group situations, I was apt to blurt out wildly inappropriate remarks, like a person with Tourette's syndrome. I cried all the time. I lost thirty pounds.

Weeks passed, then months. I was wearing out my husband and my friends. But I couldn't calm down. It was almost as if I had become addicted to these days on fire, to this intensity. I felt that if I lost it, I'd lose him even more.

Finally I started going to a psychiatrist, a kind, rumpled man who formed his hands into a little tent and listened to me scream and cry and rave for several weeks.

Then came the day when he held up his hand and said, "Enough."

"What?" I stared at him.

"I am going to give you a new prescription," my psychiatrist said, taking out his pad and pen. He began to write.

"Oh, good," I said, wanting more drugs, anything.

He ripped the prescription out and handed it to me.

"Write fiction every day," it said in his crabbed little hand.

I just looked at him.

"I have been listening to you for some time," he said, "and it has occurred to me that you are an extremely lucky person, since you are a writer, because it is possible for you to enter into a narrative not your own, for extended periods of time. To live in someone else's story, as it were. I want you to do this every day for two hours. I believe that it will be good for you."

"I can't," I said. "I haven't written a word since Josh died."

"Do it," he said.

"I can't think straight, I can't concentrate," I said.

"Then just sit in the chair," he said. "Show up for work."

Vocational rehabilitation, I thought. Like Josh. So I did it. For three days. The fourth day, I started to write.

And my novel, which I'd planned as the diary of a young girl orphaned by the Civil War, just took off and wrote itself. "I know I am a spitfire and a burden," Molly Petree begins on May 20, 1874. "I do not care. My family is a dead family, and this is not my home, for I am a refugee girl . . . but evil or good I intend to write it all down every true thing in black and white upon the page, for evil or good it is my own true life and I WILL have it. I will."

Molly's spitfire grit strengthened me as she proceeded to "give all her heart," no matter what, during a passionate life journey that included love, betrayal, motherhood, and grief (of course, grief). But by the time we were done with it, Molly and I, two years later, she had finally found a real home, and I could find my way to the grocery store. I could laugh. And yes, through the mysterious alchemy of fiction, my sweet Josh had managed to find his own way into the final pages of the novel after all, as a mystical bluesman and healer living wild and free at last in the deep piney woods he used to play in as a child.

When Joan Didion published *My Year of Magical Thinking*, with its close observation of her life during the painful year following her husband's death, a friend wondered, "How can she do that—write at such a time?"

"The right question is, how could she *not* do that?" I answered. Writing is what Joan Didion does, it's what she has always done. It's how she has lived her life.

In a different way, I realized, this is how I have lived my life, too. Of course writing is an escape, but it is a source of nourishment and strength, too. My psychiatrist's prescription may benefit us all. Whether we are writing fiction or nonfiction, journaling or writing for publication, writing itself is an inherently therapeutic activity. Simply to line up words one after another upon a page is to create some order where it did not exist, to give a recognizable shape to the chaos of our lives. Writing cannot bring our loved ones back, but it can sometimes fix them in our fleeting memories as they were in life, and it can always help us make it through the night.

On the Baton Rouge Floods of 2016 and My Nostalgia for the Half-gone

M. O. Walsh

My Aunt Debby bought the place from her mother in 1981. Originally built as a fishing camp in the 1950s, it's located right on the bank of the Amite River, about twenty miles south of Baton Rouge in the small village of Port Vincent, Louisiana. Aunt Debby has spent the last thirty-five years of her life there, having raised the foundation from 10 feet to 13.5 feet after the 1983 floods, which got her. Although we still call it "The Camp," it's actually a large and sophisticated home, into which Aunt Debby has poured her life savings. It has hardwood floors and a kitchen island, a screened-in porch with an outdoor TV, a master suite that looks over the water, a boat dock with Christmas lights. It looks nearly untouchable up there on its stilts. So much so that when the contractor finished raising it back in the eighties, he told my aunt, "If this place ever floods again, it'll mean that Baton Rouge has been completely destroyed."

On August 14, 2016, my aunt was ferried to The Camp by boat, where she cupped her eyes with her hands to look through the windows. Inside she saw water lines on her appliances. The odd rearrangement of furniture pushed around in the flow. The tracks of unseen snakes, like lost rivers, across the silted floor of her home.

◦

Eudora Welty says that fiction, of all art forms, is the one "least likely to cut the cord that binds it to its source." Flannery O'Connor, Barry Hannah—if you dig enough, you could probably find that every southern writer, present or past, has said something about the importance of place in her or his work. I have to admit, growing up in Louisiana and being inundated in that tradition, I got a little tired of it. I believed, instead, the great promise of fiction is that it is boundless, limited only by the writer's imagination. I set my earliest stories in Ohio, Montana, Detroit—all places I'd never been. I felt pretty good crossing the Mason-Dixon in my head. That was two decades ago. Those early stories remain with me still, keeping each other good company in a folder on my computer called REJECTED.

◆

The rainfall in Baton Rouge during August 1989 totaled 7.67 inches.

This is the type of easy research writers enjoy when imagining the past. I googled up similar facts when, in my thirties, I worked on a novel set in the late eighties and early nineties in my hometown. It was my first time writing about the place where I grew up, and I found myself so overwhelmed by nostalgia for Baton Rouge that I figured a little science would do me good. Inevitably, the numbers came to nothing. I remembered so clearly the way the creeks and bayous that ran behind my old neighborhood backed up in a storm, the way, as kids, we'd wade around the yard in our rain boots, paddle canoes down the street, cast fishing lines off the porch, catch the frogs that lined the water's edge. Yet I could not find any floods or named storms to match the dates on my family's photographs that showed us doing these exact things. Were these disasters, I wondered?

I was too young at the time to know the bond to place I was then making, in those moments of delight with the water-that-shouldn't-have-been-where-it-was. I was too young to know this was the same bond so many who write the South feel. I was too young, in other words, to see the future. Too young to already miss the place that I lived.

◆

This year, in the week of August 8th alone, 7.1 trillion gallons of rain fell on Louisiana. When the flooding hit Baton Rouge, the cell phone service went down. From New Orleans, where I now live, I texted both of my parents and received delayed and sporadic replies:

"Water in the street but I think we'll be ok."

"Your step-dad took the boat out this morning. Rescued 4 families."
Similar dispatches came in from Lafayette and Denham Springs. The interstate system, which connects these places, was soon underwater as well. Then pictures came through from the old neighborhood, the same neighborhood I'd spent most of the last decade writing about, water rising above the doorknobs.

I think of Zora Neale Hurston. Harper Lee. William Faulkner.

Eatonville. Maycomb County. Yoknapatawpha.

Our best writers have a way of articulating the South so that it feels, at the same time, always alive and already past. I think about rural communities giving way to strip malls. The ghosts of soldiers in blue walking across a family's well-manicured, present-day lawn. I think about my old neighborhood, a disappearing coast. I wonder if southern writers know something different than most about the ground we all stand on.

I wonder if we live, at all times, in the half-gone.

When the interstates reopened I took a trip to Baton Rouge to see my people, have a look around. I wanted to see the street I grew up on first. As I drove into the neighborhood, it seemed already restored. People were out mowing their grass, walking their dogs in the heat. Then I turned the corner to my street, stopped the car, pulled out my phone, and hit record. Every house on the block was gutted. Heirlooms lined the road like demolition hills. Piles of sheetrock and end tables, mattresses and carpeting. The buzz of flies on family freezers. The smell. The video I caught does no justice.

I parked near my old house and got out of the car. Although I hadn't lived there for nearly thirty years, I stood on the curb and sorted the ruined material as if it were my own. The front door to the house stood open and I walked inside. If I'd wanted to, I could have walked straight through the wooden framing, where there used to be walls, and into the backyard. "Hello," I said, but there was nobody home.

Yesterday, I talked to Aunt Debby on the phone. She's living with my mom, whose house in Baton Rouge was luckily spared. The water at The Camp has now receded enough for her to drive there, and she visits it every day, either with insurance adjustors or contractors or by herself to go through what cannot be saved. I was curious how she was holding up.

"Are you at your house now?" she asked me.

"Yes," I told her.

"Take out a measuring tape," she said. "Measure two and a half feet off the ground. Draw a line along the wall. Everything below that is gone."

I told her I couldn't imagine.

"You should do it," she said. "I'm serious."

"I will," I said.

"Your dressers," she said. "Your filing cabinets. Your kids' toys. Your hanging clothes. Your photo albums. All of your furniture. Your appliances. Your guitar. Everything under your bed."

"My god," I said.

"All of your shoes."

⌖

I showed my seven-year-old daughter the video I made of my old neighborhood's wreckage. She asked me which house was mine, and I told her: the white one in the corner behind that big pile of stuff. She seemed especially interested in the clip of a gang of flies crawling in and out of the vents at the bottom of a freezer that had been set on the curb and wrapped with duct tape.

"What are they doing?" she asked me.

"They're finding a way in," I told her.

"Was that your freezer?" she asked. "The one you had as a kid?"

"I don't know," I said. "I doubt it."

She looked at our own refrigerator, still new, stainless steel. This is the place she gets her food from; a crisp apple, a cup of milk. This is a thing she can count on.

"But it could have been," she said.

"Yes," I said.

I wondered if it was fear or knowledge I saw on her face at that moment. I wonder if there is a difference.

⌖

It took me forty years of life, more than twenty years of writing, to realize that a story's setting is no arbitrary thing. To write about one's home is not a sign of imaginative weakness. It is instead like having a lover or child whose true power over you is only felt when you understand that one day, possibly this very day, that person will be gone.

So, I drop to my knees and take out my measuring tape. The lawn is mowed. The A/C is humming. The paint is still fresh and bright. But I've lived here long enough to know what's coming. So I draw my line across the wall and listen for the trickle of water.

I wait for the splashing of snakes.

IV

Writing about Race

But for the national welfare, it is urgent to realize that the minorities do think, and think about something other than the race problem.
—ZORA NEALE HURSTON, AFRICAN AMERICAN (SOUTHERN) NOVELIST, SHORT STORY WRITER, FOLKLORIST, AND ANTHROPOLOGIST

The Past Is Just Another Name for Today

W. Ralph Eubanks

*S*omeone told me that once you discover the past in the present, you can understand the world. Yet the way I look at the world rests deep in a place with a sometimes tortured and tangled history, one that often creeps into contemporary life. That is why Mississippi holds talismanic qualities that inform what I write as well as the way I engage with its history. My past influences what I see within the state's borders as well as what I see outside of them. These collisions with memory confuse and surprise me, but more often than not they serve as a clarifying force, one that allows me to look forward as well as backward and see the ways the past manifests itself in my everyday life.

I'm often asked why Mississippi's civil-rights past plays such a large role in my work as a writer and editor, particularly when what I am writing is focused on the present. The short answer is that we are all products of the era that shaped us, and I feel called to witness and keep the legacy of that time alive. In response to my acts of witness and memory on the page, I was once asked, "Do you really need to keep bringing all that stuff up from the past? Isn't it painful?" My response was a resounding "yes" to both, since Mississippi's history—as well as the history of this country—is littered with the consequences of denial and cultural erasure. With respect to whether it was painful to revisit the past, I pointedly asked the questioner, "for whom is it painful?" Is it more painful for me to remember the violence that erupted all around Mississippi—violence directed at people of color like me—or is it more painful for those who listen to me tell these stories to be reminded of those who did little to stop those senseless and brutal acts? Clarity about the past rarely comes about without pain for the person remembering the past or the person encountering those recollections.

To that occasional doubter in the audience at a reading or lecture, I often note that turning a blind eye to turbulent events may seem easier than confronting them head-on, but in the long run the truth always triumphs and casts its light. It cannot be denied. This is the true burden of southern history: the past stays with you and cannot be ignored. If you disregard or deny the existence of pieces of it, it will somehow find a place to penetrate your consciousness. And the place in your psyche the past chooses to burrow down into might render discomfort deeper than the recesses of the dark loamy soil of the Mississippi Delta.

Over the years, I have come to realize that the past shapes who we are and what we become. My lived experience has taught me that turning away from one's personal history is a way of denying yourself and your very existence. Once I came to terms with this fact, I stopped keeping Mississippi at arm's length and embraced the place of my birth. In spite of my status as what I call "a born-again southerner," I maintain a skeptical eye that serves as a faithful companion to this newfound intimacy with the South. After coming back to live and work in Mississippi for a year, teaching literature and writing, I even gained a fresh perspective that sharpened my sensibilities about the connection between the past and the present. What I realized after living in Mississippi again is that it is a place that continues to be a scene and a symbol, as well as a part of the country sustained by myth and ritual. While it seems paradoxical, it is the way Mississippi continues to embrace its myths that troubles me, yet it is the deception and denial of history that also propels my writing. When I write, Mississippi speaks to me through the ages both loudly and in hushed tones I can hear when I stop and listen carefully. It is the things the place says to me quietly that capture my attention the most, since these are the things that are most likely to be forgotten and need to be woven into stories that need to be told.

But first I had to learn to listen and I had to learn ways of seeing the past. It doesn't matter where I am in the state—the Piney Woods where I grew up or in the Delta or Hill Country—something or someone I encounter will force a memory into the present. It is often a visual cue—a place or a photograph—that will push me toward a journey into the past, often one for which I have no memory.

᪣

A work of literature often begins with what the eye sees, and a photograph sometimes captures a bigger story than can be told in a single image. That is why when I am trying to connect the past and the present in my writing, I find myself turning to the dusky glow of old black-and-white or sepia images. Lately Marion Post Wolcott's 1939 photographs of Mileston, Mississippi, have helped me place where my parents lived when they first moved to the Delta. One photograph shows the old Mileston plantation store, a building that no longer exists. Today another structure sits on its footprint and occupies the landscape in a way that makes imagining the old store possible, as well as the stark reality of the Delta that greeted my parents upon their arrival from coastal Alabama. The photograph of the white clapboard building was taken before the house next to it where my parents spent their first years as a married couple was built. But the photograph captured the site where a spare wooden house eventually found its place on that flat, lonely parcel in the Delta.

I'm far too young to have any memory of the Great Depression, yet Wolcott's photographs of Depression-era images capture the Delta landscape as I once saw it. It's a reminder to me of the constancy of place in Mississippi, where the landscape in many ways remains relatively unaltered. If it is true, as Susan Sontag wrote, that photographs testify to time's relentless melt, Mississippi's landscape is filled with places that capture moments in time and freeze them in place. There are places all around the state where time only melts along the edges.

One of the places in Mississippi that seems frozen in time lies at the end of a wooded street in Oxford, Mississippi. It's hard to look at Faulkner's Rowan Oak without thinking of memory's shadow, which casts its presence as soon as the house's white columns fall into view, since Faulkner believed that memory loomed over the past and influenced the present and the future. Sometimes it seems as if this house, frozen in time, is holding the past safely in place and allowing time to click by with little intrusion from the present.

Outside of the grounds of Rowan Oak, the Oxford Faulkner knew occasionally intrudes on a visitor's consciousness. Yes, the courthouse still looms over the Square in Oxford, giving you a flavor of Faulkner's fictional Jefferson, where life was lived with that Faulknerian triumvirate of grief, fury, and despair. But little else of Faulkner's world remains in Oxford and what you can find, you have to travel deep into Mississippi's landscape and know where to look. Once I went deep into the woods of Lafayette County in search of the spot that inspired the river crossing in *As I Lay Dying*. One rainy spring afternoon a friend and I waded across a fast-moving creek and imagined the wagon carrying Addie Bundren's body trying to safely reach the other side. It was in that moment that I not only connected Faulkner's imagination to a place, but also realized how those places from the past, both real and imagined, live alongside all of us today. We can all experience the past in the present if we are willing to go deep.

The same can be said about delving into Mississippi's history. One must be willing to travel into Mississippi's cavernous psyche and its past, deeper than many are willing to travel, in order to find a connection. To some, ties to the past may seem torturous, but for me this linkage with history is my calling. Rather than being caught in the moonlit glow of nostalgia, the past helps me engage with the present with clear eyes. That is why the past no longer scares me, since now I know that the past is just another name for today.

Black Countermelodies

Ravi Howard

*I*n a sermon I heard in college, Rev. Samuel Proctor told a story from his childhood. Every evening his father, a Virginia shipyard worker, would clean the oil from his fingers and then play his violin. I was struck by the beauty of the moment he presented, showing these layers of black southern life. Through the violin, Proctor's father showed this second voice, a countermelody, a contrast from the voice and self that existed in his working life. I heard that story from Proctor when I was in college, a few years before I seriously pursued writing as a career, but I considered his words a craft lesson on the interior complexity of black characters and their voices.

This countermelody is an element that Zora Neale Hurston presents so beautifully in the opening pages of *Their Eyes Were Watching God*. She offers a vital lesson in reading the second voices that the black characters hid behind silences until they returned to the safety of their communities.

> It was the time for sitting on porches beside the road. It was the time to hear things and talk. These sitters had been tongueless, earless, eyeless conveniences all day long. Mules and other brutes had occupied their skins. But now, the sun and the bossman were gone, so the skins felt powerful and human. They became lords of sounds and lesser things. They passed nations through their mouths.

The characters Hurston gathers after sunset are employed in servitude to white families and bosses. Hurston's eloquence carries a clear message that silence was a means of self-defense from the threat of violence or lost wages in an economy with few opportunities or protections. Work is no place for truth-telling, so the truth is withheld, sometimes resonating in the interiority, a shared moment between character and reader. In her essay, "Voice and Interiority in Zora Neale Hurston's *Their Eyes Were Watching God*," Maria Rancine defines interiority as "an author's relatively full and non-judgmental rendering of the internal consciousness of a character."

Too often, in the depiction of black characters working for white families, the first voice, the voice that navigates servitude, is all the reader gets. Yes, we hear a voice and see the quotations on the page, but what about the rest of the character? Who are the characters in their private spaces? What anchors them to family and community? Where do they live when they are off the page? The voices, governed by the long history of black service and concerned with the requirements of their employers' endearment and comfort, cannot show the candor shared in the company of friends. The depth and the resonance of the countermelodies don't always appear in dialogue, making an inner voice necessary.

I remember a talk years back from Georgia poet Ed Pavlic about musicality and fidelity in lines and voices, and I still consider those concepts. The music and truth often reside in the interiority of characters. However, instead of being seen as fidelity, that depth can be dismissed as inauthentic. In a 2014 *Guernica* interview, Jesmyn Ward spoke about the resistance she encountered when she created complex interior voices in her work.

> When I was working on *Salvage*, I would get feedback that the difference was too wide—between the characters' speech, where I'm using dialect or colloquial language, and their thoughts, which are smart and complicated. But that's something I learned from Faulkner. In Faulkner's work, people speak one way, but then they're allowed to have interior lives expressed with ten-dollar words because those are the words that best represent a person's rich, complicated emotions.

Ward's 2011 National Book Award for *Salvage the Bones* was an important moment in southern fiction, because her young protagonist, Esch, challenges the narrow view of the authentic black southern voice. Esch's fascination with mythology brought Jason and Medea into her mind, sharing space with her hardships and aspirations in rural, Gulf Coast Mississippi. The cycle of the real and imagined moments created a vividness in the visual storytelling and the voices that resounded through the novel.

In her essay *Site of Memory*, Toni Morrison notes her interest in the interior lives and sees that develop as a way "to explore two worlds—the actual and the possible." Perhaps the two-worlds concept was ingrained in Morrison in her childhood experience as a house cleaner. In an interview with the *Guardian*, she recounts the time her white employer complained about her cleaning skills, and Morrison asked her father for advice. "'Go to work, get your money and come home. You don't live there.' She was not obliged, he said, to live as they saw her in their imagination."

The concept of living in the imagination of others has been important in my research and work, because I've tried to develop the dual voices, especially for characters in the public eye. I have been drawn to musicians and their voices as a writer, reader, and a fan of a good song. I was interested in the sound, the public voice, but also the voice away from the microphone. The duality of the black voices, with a public and private component, was a standard of the entertainment world. The persona clicked off and on long enough for that public voice to resonate on stage or on record. Likewise, black workers, like the ones in my family and those I've known, have noted that service work required a kind of staging common in entertainment. They were expected to play a role, or as Paul Laurence Dunbar called it, to "wear the mask."

In his novel *Dancing in the Dark*, Caryl Phillips follows the lives of popular blackface vaudeville performers, including the husband and wife team George and Aida Walker, around the turn of the twentieth century. When the Walkers and their partner Bert Williams stage a show without blackface, they defy the expectations of their audience and face a severe backlash in the press, prompting Aida to write a response to their critics in the *New York Times*. "There are ten thousand things we must think of every time we make a step and I am not sure that the public is fully aware of the limitations which other persons have made on us." The writing is compelling because of the ratio, one step versus ten thousand things. With so much ground to cover in the interior, that space requires development on the page.

The tensions that Walker described are well established in the voices and silences of historical characters, but novels like *Queen Sugar* show contemporary versions. Natalie Baszile develops a compelling model of the depth beneath the tongueless mouths that Hurston describes. Prosper Denton, a retired cane farmer, has agreed to help Charlie Bordelon, a young woman who has left Los Angeles to run her late father's struggling sugarcane farm in Louisiana. While at an auction, Denton runs into Samuel Landry, his former employer, a man who dominates the local sugarcane community. As Landry offers insults wrapped in smiles, Denton becomes silent. Charlie is disheartened as Denton shrinks into himself. The tension is clear. The pair can't afford new equipment, so the auction is their only option.

In an act of spite, Landry bids up the prices on equipment Charlie and Denton need—an act of spite, not necessity. Denton, instead of raising the auction paddle or saying a word, disappears into the crowd, and Charlie believes he's left. As the auction ends and the crowd leaves, Charlie finds Denton. His second voice was personified in an accomplice. The friend, an alternative, secret voice, secured the equipment needed for the farm to continue. Denton's meekness was a performance, and success was only possible on the other side of silence.

Baszile accomplishes something that is compelling. The conversation between the former black worker and the white landowner is shown without romance or nostalgia. During his time as an employee, Denton's labor may have been valued, but that value, and any respect, had a ceiling. As a peer, the relationship changes, and that contemporary tension carries the residue of our racial history.

In historical fiction, the dialogue of the black servant is often a negotiation. Characters barter to remain employed and to stay in the good graces of those with economic power. Candor would have upset an already delicate balance, leading to financial hardship and even violence. So the interior voice, wrapped in silence, gives the characters the distance to live and maneuver.

In *Letters to a Young Poet*, Rainer Maria Rilke encourages the "turn inward" and the "descent into your inner self and into your secret place of solitude." I've considered those notes in the context of character development. The inward turn serves as the only available exodus or migration for stifled black characters. Brit Bennett chronicles a similar turn in *The Mothers*, with a medley of silences that the characters chronicle. "We left the world. Each in her own time and way," Bennet writes, equating this silent retreat to death or a spiritual exodus required to endure indignities. "We tried to love the world. We cleaned after this world, scrubbed its hospital floors and ironed its shirts, sweated in its kitchens and spooned school lunches, cared for its sick and nursed its babies. But the world didn't want us, so we left. . . ."

This migration, into the refuge of the interior, gives depth to characters and adds texture to their silences. As readers and writers, we map their migration from the world around them to the world within. The older women in Bennett's work found a means of escape. For many, the Great Migration offered safe passage, while others had to create the interior journey. In *The Warmth of Other Suns*, Isabel Wilkerson offers a telling scene of the first and second voice in conversation. She tells the story of Henry Brown, who mails himself to freedom in a box. After a treacherous journey, an accomplice waits for the container, afraid that Brown has died in transit. Wilkerson describes the exchange between the two voices. "'Is all right within?' the voice asked, trembling. 'All right,' Brown replied. The people were joyful. And Brown was free."

Henry Brown's box represents that interior space, with one voice in the world and another concealed until a moment when he could both live and speak freely. The countermelody serves as a call and response. That pattern repeated on the porch where Hurston's ensemble gathered with "nations passing through their mouths." Those nations, those other worlds, carry the questions and answers that could only be asked by the voice carried within.

All That "Southern" Jazz

Claude Wilkinson

*N*ow about the South, even the boys in my community who had never heard of a creative writing class, nor who were ever promoted as far as high school for that matter, were still master storytellers in their own right. Their syntax was always impeccably ungrammatical and their inflections always mood-swingingly hip. Each added his own riff to already mythic standards, such as "The Preacher and the Bear," "The Signifying Monkey," and most popular of all, "Shine," the tale of a heroic black stoker who constantly violated racial taboos and bested manipulative white folk. When we reached the part where the ship went down, some boys' Shine outswam a shark, some's outswam a whale, just like a swarthy double to Beowulf might. Some boys' Shine ignored the drowning bargain of white women's favors, while some's first took advantage before swimming off, their variations probably guided by each teller's predilection.

In his poem "Dark Prophecy: I Sing of Shine," Mississippi-born poet Etheridge Knight treats the legend with an equally funky but cosmopolitan flair, so that Shine alone ends up having swum many miles of icy ocean to the pleasures of the big city, and is partying in Harlem long before any news of his ship's sinking makes it ashore. But one didn't begin with this high-wire dervish of trying to crack up a jury of calloused judges who had given an ear to so many versions of the same tale before because if you missed a note or a line fell flat, other boys' successes would be paraded in front of you like a hall of fame you hadn't achieved: "You ought to heard my second cousin tell it," or "When Pee Wee be tellin' it, he say. . . ." No, one needed to hone this craft in a more intimate setting—wordplay we called jonin'.

This was a generally good-natured assault on another's hygiene, his appearance, his lack of smarts or wherewithal. All the better if one's sparring partner showed some conceived imperfection like raggedy teeth or grungy feet to zero in on. And in our neck of the woods, this wasn't to be confused with playing the dozens, which was a more serious venture. Jonin' usually ended when one opponent gained the most raucous laugh for his insults, while the dozens, because they tackled weightier topics like another's mama's questionable virtue, often ended in fights. But was any of this exclusively southern, or the grounds of its occurrence holy to my path as a writer? While our traditions seemed communal to us at the time, they had surely migrated among other black folk who had never set foot in the South.

Only after being asked a good many years later to guest-edit a literary journal's special issue on southern poetry did I begin pondering whether such a subgenre existed. From early on, I had read Knight and Robert Penn Warren faithfully, but I'd never really considered either's poems in terms of their southernness. Reading fiction, on the other hand, was a different matter. It usually appeared as if such adept writers as William Faulkner and Barry Hannah were brandishing one of those distorting mirrors when they told about the South. I mean, in what other world is one likely to find believable an atheistic Bible salesman who steals a woman's glass eye and a girl's prosthetic leg simply because the objects interest him, as happens in Flannery O'Connor's "Good Country People"? But when I began to wonder what, if anything, would make a poem or poet, myself included, expressly southern, I found I needed to first consider what makes a place seem southern to me.

In my tenure as the Grisham Writer in Residence at Ole Miss, a movement arose to finally scrap the state's archaic Confederate flag, and during an ensuing furor, I spied on some Oxonian's rust bucket a sticker boasting, "If I had known all this, I would've picked my own cotton!" That felt southern. When I now drive past the third-generation Wadsworth Clinic in Hernando, Mississippi, on my way to the library or the barbershop, and remember the waiting room's antiseptic smell and inferred color line that was carefully maintained throughout my early childhood, this too still feels southern. During a conversation with a young, leadfoot grad student assigned to be my driver, somewhere along the highway from Albuquerque on the way to Santa Fe, where I was to conduct a poetry workshop, she observed, "Sounds to me like you have a love/hate relationship with Mississippi."

"I don't know about the love part anymore," I quipped.

Yet in the same Wadsworth Clinic, I remember a white woman sitting on that side giving up her spot in line as my mother frantically cradled me after a rather serious injury suffered while playing in our yard, and this feels southern too. Though through the rosy glass of retrospect, it seems my love was mostly for that amazing space. Black families' properties connected as seamlessly and prophetically for my wandering and latent inspiration as Ezekiel's dry bones: Mr. Bill Malone's place joined to that of my grandmother, whom most people called Aunt Babe; Aunt Babe's land connected with Mr. Elie Anderson's; Mr. Elie's homestead was right across a narrow dirt road from Mr. Lucius Williams's, and so on. I was the child of blackberry thickets, wild muscadines, and golden persimmons. Fences were mainly there to keep livestock in, and as long as there was no mean bull inside, and you didn't steal watermelons, or get caught swimming in anyone's pond, it was like being loosed in a promised land.

My friend Isaac Chung, who is a filmmaker now living near Los Angeles, was reared in the Ozark Mountains, so we sometimes joke about how Mississippi and Arkansas always seem to be jockeying for last place when it comes to anything progressive. That's not to say I don't bristle like a watchdog when outsiders attack. I've had to set a Big Apple dweller or two's soup outside, as my mother used to put it.

As for my boundaries for the journal's southern issue, I decided to include writers or writing that had ties to any of the fourteen recognized southern states. Just how "southern" did it end up being? The range of poems submitted and finally selected ran the gamut from those with extraordinarily long titles that mimicked clichéd southern names, and alluded to homespun locations, churchgoing, and the working-class poor to a ritualistic farewell of a Chinese father to his son after the son is killed by an earthquake in Sichuan; from poets who had merely moved to the region for jobs to those who had been southerners all their lives. So what distinguished those who were born and bred? Conditions, language? Well, a poet who isn't an original southerner wrote of being broke, trying to hire herself out as a char, while some poets who were dyed-in-the-wool southerners versed their take on ecology without any references to treeing coons or skinning a buck—in short, nothing so gothic as the caricature of southern fiction nowadays.

To be fair, myth and stereotypes don't always come out of the blue. Some southerners drawl, some are unlearned, and some, no doubt, have married close kin. But are even any of these traits necessarily southern? Another friend, a writer and musician also living in L.A., and I don't talk often now, but when we do, we always recommend books, music, and movies to each other. Once, some years ago, I told her about a comedy's hilarious scene that parodied the film *Deliverance,* as an unwary appliance salesman stumbles lost through woods upon an inbred Appalachian household and is greeted with *Deliverance's* infamous pizzicato of dread played by twin nose- and banjo-picking boys. Through muffled laughter, my friend, a native North Carolinian, objected, "I hate Hollywood."

Of course, southern views on religion, particularly Christianity, are also usually depicted at best as unique, but are often skewed through the prism of cinema and literature, even, perhaps especially, by southerners themselves. On a Christmas visit, my brother-in-law described a sign he had seen on the semitrailer of an eighteen-wheeler while traveling from Decatur, Georgia, to Rienzi, Mississippi. The sign read: "Jesus. You better know him before you have to meet him. Stop, drop, and roll don't work in Hell!" I can just imagine Flannery O'Connor's eyes becoming as big as bo dollars with ideas for a story if she had seen such. Possibly my favorite fiction writer, she seemingly examined as many fervid interpretations of religiosity as her short time allowed.

If there is a seal on southerners that identifies them as peculiar to all other people, it's quite likely our spiritualness. At a southern lit seminar, I once engaged a routinely pompous professor when he vehemently denied any biblical symbolism in Richard Wright's haiku. Granted, every mention of a snake, even when called "serpent" or "viper," may not be the repressed pain of having lost Eden surfacing. And just because sparrows are often Wright's bird of choice doesn't mean that we'll find "God's eye is on" spelled backward anywhere among the seventeen syllables. But it's hard to believe one could ever be free of the indelible background of religion that *Black Boy* recounts. Whether a true southerner opposes, straddles, or embraces upbringing to do with religion, it's always wrestled with. O'Connor's characters never escape it, and neither do we.

Of the five poems in which I mention snakes in *Reading the Earth,* my first collection, only once is a snake meant just to be a snake. Curiously, though, readers often placed the weight of their attention on my metaphors of the natural world rather than on the spiritual realm they sought to explain, or at least explore. Other poems in the book offer droves of chattering blackbirds that point to the obedience of Joshua at the walls of Jericho; cardinals gingerly lighting in a Christ's thorn bringing to mind the crucifixion; and the tiniest of spiders spinning a web strong enough to trap sunlight, as a morality of strength in weakness and the meek inheriting the earth. Without the poems' prevalent inclination toward belief, all they might reveal is a patient way of looking, and the spider in my poem could just as easily be a metaphor for doubt as the spider in "Design" by New Englander Robert Frost. In other words, while readers sifted to find idiomatic expressions, or terrain they could hoist as qualities of southernness in my poems, it seems to me, they overlooked a litmus test of spirituality.

Then too, there's always been the music—mainly the blues, which belongs to Mississippi, then to the South, then to Chicago, and to the rest of the world, in that order. Yet as much as I love it, blues per se seldom shows up in my poetry. Though a reviewer did remark that my poems carried the wisdom and feel of the blues. Mississippi native Sterling Plumpp, a noted "blues poet," and I have never shot the breeze about southern, nor even any American, poets, as far as I recall. Professor emeritus at an Illinois university, he left the state a long time ago, so it's hardly common ground. But don't let one of us bring up Son House, Skip James, Sam Chatmon, or Bukka White! I've always loved spirituals too, but as for blues and gospel's southern children, only in recent years have I warmed nicely to jazz and become less chilly toward zydeco.

Oh yes, and there's that other southern thing we do as well, perhaps especially writers, maybe most especially Mississippi writers—you know that balancing act we've taught ourselves: to presume to trade on the proud fellowship of genius alongside Margaret Walker, Tennessee Williams, Eudora Welty, et cetera—while secretly wishing you were from somewhere else. Whether in the United States or abroad, I don't think I've ever been asked where I was from without suspecting that hidden behind the inquisition, a disdainful opinion is lurking to pounce. As I wrote in the introduction for the journal's southern poetry issue that I edited, I was asked the question by two European men on a train in Wales. After answering, "Mississippi," one of them added, "Nothing worse than Mississippi, eh."

And once at Atlanta's Hartsfield airport, a baggageman impertinently asked, "So where you from, Claude?" My first thought was to tell him I was from Paris, in French, so as to curtly end his inquiry, but then there was that lying and religion creature and what not, rearing their incongruous, inconvenient heads again. And there was also the probability that had he somehow found out the truth, my luggage would've ended up in Honolulu instead of in Memphis with me. As soon as I'd urged the truth, the baggageman struck: "I thought so. *Claude*, that's a country name." My next impulses were quickly loaded like rounds in a tommy gun: "What do you consider to be 'country'?" "Not all of Mississippi is rural. There are cities there too." "Actually, my name is Latin." "I didn't say I was born or named in Mississippi!" Instead, I checked the elastic on my claim tag and headed for an escalator.

In "And Tell Me Poet, Can Love Exist in Slavery?," another Knight poem, an apparently omniscient persona asks the rhetorical question of poets, and maybe even of poetry itself. "Not exactly" is the implied answer. Sean Sexton, a friend as well as a fellow poet and painter, after years of our discussing literature, great paintings, and our own techniques, proposed that he and I have a two-man show at an art museum in Florida, his home state. Since the museum's director was interested in playing up our differences and similarities for an exhibition catalog, he and I began reviewing them in a more critical light. We didn't spend superfluous time on his being white and my being black and the opposing worlds those inheritances create. What we solved is that having been reared on farms, our aesthetic became blissfully marked by our connections to the land.

For nearly three decades, I've been bending the ear of family and friends with my pipe dream of moving to Maine. The friend Isaac asked, "What about the winters?" And Jane, the writer/musician, in her typically surgical fashion, interposed, "Yeah, that Frost swinging on birches shit sounds cool and all, I just found living in New England lonely and depressing." But Sean pleaded, "Aren't you afraid of losing your muse?" My life without art was a much more solemn consideration. One mind told me it would look foolish to stop counting on leaving now since for so many years it's been my only remedy. But the blurb on one of my books says, "Claude Wilkinson is bonded to the southern landscape and deeply in love with it." I could tell Sean that nothing more than a few word choices and the look of the places I aimed to describe were apt to change. I'd have time to mull over my answer to myself later. But also lodged in my thoughts, there was that other piece making me out to be Mississippi's Thoreau.

At St. John's College in Santa Fe, in addition to my poetry workshop, I was to also give a reading. After being introduced and taking the podium, I thumbed through possibilities of failing at and being failed by faith, of an inherited burden of original sin, of being uplifted by a vision presumed in the shapes of some clouds. I read of baptisms presided over by snakes, of whippoorwills invoking prayer in the night, of strained family relations, read of growing older, and yes, often of death. Chatting later on with the only African American among my workshop students, she said that the whole while I'd stood before the audience calmly reading my grammatical poems filled with the tranquility of lightning bugs and autumn flowers, one thought kept popping up in her head. Pennsylvania-raised, and Sarah Lawrence–educated mind you, but of Kentucky descent, she confided, "I don't know why, but for some reason I couldn't stop thinking, *I wouldn't like to play the dozens with him.*" Do tell.

V

On the Craft of Writing

A story is a way to say something that can't be said any other way,
and it takes every word in the story to say what the meaning is.
—FLANNERY O'CONNOR

Three "One Things": An Essay on Writing Fiction

Clyde Edgerton

THE FIRST ONE THING

An oil painter paints a tree on a canvas. Later you look at the paint on the canvas while your mind sort of says you are seeing a tree. You realize, of course, that you aren't seeing a tree. An illusion has been created. But if the painter is good enough, you may be surprised, even delighted that the painting has triggered a satisfying kind of belief that you are looking at a tree, a tree that seems interesting.

A flick of orange-yellow paint that represents reflected light on the tree trunk may be the "one thing" that makes the painting pop for you. Perhaps, without that flick of orange-yellow, the painting would not be satisfying or convincing, but plain and dull.

With the flick of yellow-orange or some other technique, the painting comes alive; it smokes; it strikes you. Seems far more "real" than otherwise. You come to love the painting in large part because of that particular technique in that particular painting. The "one thing" has delivered—has caused success and delight.

When you are writing fiction, you are creating an illusion not unlike a painter creates an illusion. You use tricks, or I should say: you use craft to make your fiction work. As needed, you may rely on the "one thing" to strengthen your writing.

Let's go back to the tree for a second, the illusion of a tree painted by the painter. Let's say painter A paints the tree very realistically. The painting is photograph-like. But nobody stops to observe it. Yes, it's accurate . . . but uninspiring. Painter B gets the flick right and viewer after viewer loves the painting, some knowing why, some not.

One way to think about the concept of the one thing in writing was told by Chekhov this way (paraphrased): "Don't go on and on about moonlight; show me the glint of moonlight on a piece of broken green glass." If you get the one thing right, the entire scene may come clearly into the reader's head.

Now . . . I hope I've practiced the one thing guideline from my first novel on, but only recently have I been thinking about it and trying to teach the concept in isolation to my students. I've never gone through an entire revision thinking only about "the one thing" and making needed changes. My job in this essay, at this moment (I suddenly realize), is to grab a novel of mine off the shelf, open to a scene in the middle of the book, and see if what I read seems to support the "one thing" concept. I promise I will do exactly this, and if my strategy fails, you will never read these last few sentences.

At this moment, thinking aloud about which novel to pick, I realize that first-person point of view (a single character is talking to you throughout the story) is a little tricky in that the person narrating would need to be good at "the one thing," and surely not all your first-person characters will be talented in this way. In fact, some may be pointedly untalented at even getting to the point of what they are trying to say . . . so I'll refine my presentation in this essay to narratives written in third person (he, she, they, it). In third, the author generally has more control of scene description. I'll choose the last book I wrote in third person, *The Bible Salesman*. (Now, I'm doubting myself. First person narrative should, in its own way, work within a kind of "one thing" concept, but that's another essay.)

Here's the piece of a scene that I find at the top of page 119 (there are 238 pages in the hardback edition) of my novel *The Bible Salesman*. The main character, Henry Dampier, has just walked onto a front porch. He's selling Bibles.

. . . He knocked, stepped back a few steps. A lady with a hair bun on top and crochet needles stuck through it answered the door. She was bent a little. As she pushed open the screen, Henry removed his hat and held it across his stomach. He noticed that she had a little mole on her chin that looked like the tip end of a fishing worm. She had a twinkle in her eye, and held a white table napkin in her hand. He felt confident about an easy sell or two. "Oh gosh, ma'am, I'm awful sorry to be pulling you away from your dinner."

Hmm. What do you think? I think the writer perhaps used a few too many "one things." What then would be most important, most striking? I like "She was bent a little." This may be the one best one thing, in part because it helps the reader reach the conclusion that the woman is old without the writer having to use the word "old."

This piece of a scene could have been trimmed to read like this:

He knocked, stepped back a few steps. A lady with a hair bun on top and crochet needles stuck through it answered the door. She was bent a little. She held a white table napkin in her hand. "Oh gosh, ma'am," said Henry. "I'm awful sorry to be pulling you away from your dinner."

But I really like the mole sentence. It brings you, visually, right in on the woman's face—a close-up (we're getting into movie language). So we have this option:

He knocked, stepped back a few steps. A lady with a hair bun on top answered the door. She was bent a little and had a little mole on her chin that looked like the tip end of a fishing worm. She held a white table napkin in her hand. "Oh gosh, ma'am," said Henry, "I'm awful sorry to be pulling you away from your dinner."

May I go off subject? I'm not sure I needed "in her hand." Why? Because the reader will do the work of placing the napkin in her hand without the writer putting it there. Also, I don't need the adjective "little" in front of "mole." I'm thinking most moles are about the same size.

Back on subject: My original paragraph may be too long—slightly too many "one things." Back off subject: I stole the "tip end of a fishing worm" idea from Larry Brown. He writes about a character with a mole that looks like a butterbean in his story "Samaritans." I loved that metaphor and set about to match it in my scene. I remember looking for a place to do that throughout the first half of *The Bible Salesman.* My making a contest with Larry Brown may have contributed to that paragraph being overloaded. In any case, if my editor had suggested I remove the mole reference, I think I would have said no. But could it be argued that the fishing worm insert is an example of an excessive uniqueness that distracts? Flannery O'Connor warned young writers about getting too "poetic" in fiction. Was I too poetic with the fishing worm metaphor? So much depends on the reader—another subject for another essay.

Now that I've wandered widely into my own fiction, and demonstrated what might have been failure in the example I dug up, let me talk about how I normally *teach* this concept of the "one thing." Forget for a moment how I might *not* practice it. (The preacher's daughter stood up tall in the congregation one Sunday morning and announced that her father had been drunk the night before. The preacher then said, "How many times do I have to tell you people: don't do what I *do*. Do what I *say* do.")

⌀

I had a boyhood friend named Joe Jackson. As a grown man, having finished his Navy duty, Joe told me how he learned to light a match in a thirty-knot wind on the deck of a ship at sea. He showed me how to do it. It's a creative act involving holding a match between the index and third finger, striking the match, and then cupping the hands so that the flame is protected inside the cup from wind. Learning about lighting a match in a thirty-knot wind taught me a lesson about writing. Joe could have told me of several Navy adventures, of the places he'd gone, sights he'd seen. Let's assume for a minute that he did tell me those things. Of all his talk, the most memorable tale would be about lighting a match in a thirty-knot wind, more specifically, his teaching me how to do the same, after telling me he learned it in the Navy.

I've had friends who were in the Navy, Army, and Air Force. But none of them related a "one thing" that stuck with me like Joe's match-lighting story and exhibition. That one thing, for me, encamped Joe Jackson in the US Navy far better than a list of particulars could have.

Before teaching my students in class how to light a match in a thirty-knot wind (sometimes we try it outside), I tell them the Joe Jackson story. I tell them if they want a fictional character to tell a convincing story about being in the Navy, one like the light-a-match-in-a-thirty-knot-wind story might be the only one needed, and given its uniqueness and clarity, it might be the right one.

THE SECOND ONE THING

We've been talking loosely about the "one thing," the one defining thing about a character (or place, or situation) in a scene or a piece of a scene. I'd like to use the above meeting-at-the-screen-door scene from *The Bible Salesman* to talk about another kind of "one thing," and that is the one-person-to-a-paragraph guideline. Here's a beginning place near the start of the several-page scene about Henry and a couple of elderly women. It begins at the bottom of page 118:

> It was good to get under the porch roof, out of the heat. He knocked, stepped back a few steps. A lady with a hair bun on top and crochet needles stuck through it answered the door. She was bent a little. As she pushed open the screen, Henry removed his hat and held it across his stomach. He noticed that she had a little mole on her chin that looked like the tip end of a fishing worm. She had a twinkle in her eye, and held a white table napkin in her hand. He felt confident about an easy sell or two. "Oh gosh, ma'am, I'm awful sorry to be pulling you away from your dinner."
>
> "Oh, I don't mind. What's your bidness?"

In the above two paragraphs I slaughtered a guideline I normally follow. I teach that writers should keep single characters in a single paragraph—a second "one thing" notion. Often I read a student-written paragraph that has more than one person in it and is consequently a bit confusing. So I'm forever saying, "Keep a single character in each paragraph—don't run the characters together in the same paragraph." If I were carefully following that guidance with the above material, I might re-work it so that it reads something like this:

> It was good to get under the porch roof, out of the heat. He knocked, stepped back a few steps.
>
> A lady with a hair bun on top and crochet needles stuck through it answered the door. She was bent a little and held a white table table napkin in her hand. She pushed open the screen. She had a twinkle in her eye. A little mole on her chin looked like the tip end of a fishing worm.

Henry removed his hat and held it across his stomach. He felt confident about an easy sell or two. "Oh gosh, ma'am, I'm awful sorry to be pulling you away from your dinner."

"Oh, I don't mind," she said. "What's your bidness?"

In the above you are with only one person per paragraph. The reader does not get mixed up. And yet, as I said, I slaughtered that guideline rule in the final version of one paragraph atop page 119 in *The Bible Salesman* above. Why? Why would I break my own rule? Hell, I don't know. Maybe I made a mistake. Maybe the version just above is better than the original. What do you think?

I'm going to argue for the original. I think maybe I wanted the reader somewhat submerged in the interplay of impressions and talk between two people. I wanted the reader to assume what each character was learning while the interplay was happening—I wanted things a little mixed up, plus I was writing from only one point of view—Henry's—and that made it a little more sensible to stay in one paragraph. I think if I were also getting into the head of the woman for some interiority I would have needed to separate out the paragraphs.

In a wandering (or "comprehensive") third-person point of view, the reader is in one character's head and then, suddenly, in another's. The rule of thumb KEEP PEOPLE UNTO THEIR OWN PARAGRAPHS (especially in dialogue) is then even more applicable.

I'll copy the second half of page 119, final version, here to show what I mean about keeping people in their own paragraphs, especially in dialogue. We take up just after the initial encounter at the door screen. The woman says,

"Oh, I don't mind. What's your bidness?"

"My name is Henry Dampier, and I'm proud to be of Christian service to you. I've got something very pretty in this little box here that I'd like to show you if you've got a minute or two, but I tell you what, ma'am—I'm going to sit right here on this porch until you finish your meal, and then I'll show you what I've got. I'm in no hurry at all."

"You come on in," she said. "It's mighty hot out here. We got a fan on inside."

"It's been hot up in North Carolina too, where I'm from. And dry. It got so dry my uncle ate three acres' worth of corn in one sitting."

"What's that?"

"It's hot and dry up in North Carolina."

"Come on in and get you a bite to eat and a glass of ice tea, if you're a mind." She pushed open the screen door all the way. "Pleased to meet you Mr. . . . what was the name?"

"Henry Dampier."

"I'm Eloise Finley. Pleased to meet you."

If *three* characters are talking, as they will be soon, it's all the more important to give each character a separate paragraph. (There are always exceptions. Several characters may be, for example, talking at once, or involved in a fight in such a way that their thoughts, words, and deeds need jumbling into a single paragraph.) The goal, regardless of technique, is to keep the reader from being distracted by anything not directly related to the meaning of the story.

THE THIRD ONE THING

As you will notice above, my bottom half of page 119 was made up of a stretch of dialogue. Sometimes writers are nervous about letting the reader listen to only talk, without being told what one or more characters are thinking. The third one thing is to, when possible, let your characters, through their talk, provide information, nuance, insight, without you, the writer, wandering around in their heads. I like to let my characters work for me, to talk along to each other without the reader knowing their thoughts, so that the reader, *without being told*, is unconsciously learning three distinct truths: 1) truths about character one, 2) truths about character two, and 3) truths about their relationships to each other and to others perhaps. If you read through what Henry and Mrs. Finley say to each other during the last half of page 119 you will notice that you are learning a good bit about each person, and about their relationship to each other—without the writer putting you inside either's head. The characters do the talking and the reader learns through their talk that it's a very warm summer day, that they are both friendly, both want to please, that neither dislikes the other, that Henry has a playful sense of humor, but is not pushy with it, that he's patient, that Mrs. Finley can't hear very well, and so on.

There are times when a writer must tell. But showing through dialogue can score a lot of points.

ALL THREE "ONE THINGS"

When revising a novel or story, it's usually helpful to read through the entire manuscript, looking for any distraction that jumps at you. Fix those, and then read through several times again, each time looking for only one kind of distraction or problem (this is actually a forth "one thing" but I'm running out of room). I'm suggesting three potential read-throughs with these questions serving as guides:

1. Do you overdo a scene, or character, or place, or analysis, or summary, or impression? Are you excessively unique in your descriptions? If so, you may need to think about the one thing principle. Let one thing make your point, your description, your character, your action.
2. Do you have paragraphs in which you mix in too many people? Consider giving each character a separate paragraph unless you are looking for a mixing of personalities or impressions. One character, one paragraph for that character.
3. Do you write down a lot about what characters are thinking in your final drafts? Get out of your characters' heads; get out of analyzing what a character means, or means to mean, or hopes, or wishes. Just let people say things to other people and write down what they say. Play with that, work on it, and if you get the dialogue right, then the reader can figure out much of what needs to be known. Then the reader is participating in the art of the story.

We all know that there are exceptions to any writing rules. Good art doesn't follow a set of stiff mandates. But you can possibly simplify, focus, unify, and pack some new punch into your writing by thinking through a few one things.

Capturing the Essence of Difference

Niles Reddick

ome years ago, my wife Michelle and I were walking in a wooded area and talking with Anne Cohen Richards, a former psychology professor and mentor who had been a student of Maslow. As we walked by a large oak tree, hundreds of yellow butterflies took flight from bushes and fluttered about us. It was a small moment in time, just a few minutes, and one of the most beautiful experiences I've ever had, and one I've never forgotten. It's analogous to capturing the essence of difference for creative writing. We experience hundreds, maybe thousands, of things all around us on a daily basis, but it's that which is uniquely different that registers on our radars the most, and that difference is what I tend to focus on when I am developing a character, describing a place, telling a story, or writing dialogue.

I think at some level, all of us are always aware of difference: in sex, race, religion, human appearance, material things, and so on. Differences in these areas are all obviously important and are an integral part of human experience. They even come to be integrated and seen as a normal part of our reality. From a writing perspective, however, there are experiences that appear as uniquely different, not part of that usual or integrated difference. Like the butterflies, the essence of the experience is often so unusual and fleeting that our creativity wants to capture it and share it with others, whether in storytelling or writing.

The first time my perception shifted and I became aware of this essence of difference was as an undergraduate student, and no, it wasn't in a class. It was in the boys' dormitory on a southern university campus. The concrete block hallway that smelled like sour socks was lined with small rooms filled with guys from all over the South, and the most popular pastime wasn't studying science, writing English essays, or even memorizing history. The most popular thing to do was flush the toilets while guys were in showers, which resulted in a scalding of hot water. The second most popular thing to do was gather in small groups in different rooms, drink beer, and tell stories. There were the daily stories of class—of who gave a particular grade (instead of having earned it), of who to take and who not to take for a class, of how a faculty member was an atheist and liberal—but most of the stories were of high school football games, dates and sexual conquests, or killing ten-point bucks in the deer woods of the South. Occasionally, guys shared ghost, religious, or family stories. It became clear that while most of the stories were nonfiction, they were all embellished in some form or fashion.

Though many of the stories were similar in character, plot, and setting, every once in a while something stood out as different. It wasn't until I told part of a story from my own family that I realized that it was so different from them, and most people actually, that I should never forget it and write about it one day. To me, the story was just another one of the typical stories from my relatives, a large eccentric family sprinkled around rural southern Georgia, relatives who had been some of the first immigrants to the state in the 1730s and had acquired large parcels of land, but had lost it all over time. The story was about one of my aunts who collected road kill and made art.

After I told a few of my dorm friends about my aunt and her hobby, they were laughing, coughing, and wiping tears. It became crystal clear for me that I had a different sort of relative than most, an aunt who not only hacked off deer legs to use for legs of a table, but skinned dead rattlesnakes to make belts, used the snake bones to make jewelry, and removed a raccoon skin from a fresh kill along the interstate to make a toilet seat cover, just to name a few of her creations. These behaviors were all very odd and in a time before recycling had become the popular thing to do, but this wasn't my aunt's only odd behavior. She saved the small remains of mostly used-up bars of soap and collected them in a giant pickle jar she'd convinced the convenience store manager to give her once they sold all the pickles (it may have taken a few years before they had all sold). She also made wine, which was a bit more akin to moonshine (this incidentally, was not all that different an experience than most of my friends' relatives). One of the strangest was her belief in peroxide. The chemical make-up of peroxide has an extra atom of oxygen compared to the make-up of water, and she believed we needed the extra oxygen because of all the pollution in the world. So, my aunt put it in her tea, which caused it to fizz. At family reunions, all of the relatives who drank the tea were getting extra oxygen, except me. I feared for my life and felt guilty for not sharing my insider knowledge with them, though none of them ever got sick or died.

As the years passed, I wrote another story about my aunt when she developed dementia. In her last couple of years of life, she fell in love with and carried on long conversations with the director of the local funeral home whose picture was on a handheld paper fan she used. A dashing fellow poised in a dark suit on a cherry desk, the funeral home director was stationary. He always had a smile for my aunt no matter what she said. The irony, of course, was that she eventually went to be with him, literally.

I've often heard that in the South, we don't hide crazy; we put it out on the front porch or sometimes even in the yard for everyone to see. While that is tongue and cheek, it does illustrate that to capture the essence of what is different and unique in the South is to offer a new canvas in our art, and that is exactly what I have done in my own writing and what I often encourage my students and audiences to do. In the example of my aunt, it was character and behavior, but with other stories, it's the story itself or even language.

I recently wrote a small flash fiction piece titled "Wet Nurse" that was based on my paternal grandmother who had been a wet nurse for several people in a small rural community in the South. I never had heard that until a woman came up to me at a funeral and told me my grandmother had saved her life, that my grandmother had fed her when she was starving. I was surprised because my grandmother hadn't worked outside the home, never drove a car, and mostly walked to a small church near her home. In fact, when the lady said she saved her life, I figured she beat her to salvation with her Bible like she did the rest of us. The only deviant behavior I had ever heard about from my paternal grandmother was when she and her best friend had tried a can of beer when they were in their mid-seventies. After driving to the edge of their dry county, buying a single can at "the county line" liquor store, pulling off into a cornfield, and sitting on the hood of her friend's blue Ford Galaxy, they split the beer between them. All the grandchildren got the anti-alcohol lecture, how she and her friend threw up in the cornfield, how it was of the devil. She also believed television was of the devil, that the government filmed the moon landing in Hollywood to turn us away from God. After this year's political dramas, I wonder if my grandmother was partly right.

When I finally sent some of my older cousins an email query, they confirmed our grandmother had not only served as a wet nurse, she had also healed herself and others by using afterbirth. I could accept the wet nurse story even though I found it difficult to imagine my grandmother had fed just anyone's baby, but she did—as if her Christian milk would save them from their own eventual sinful demise—but the afterbirth seemed odd. She had healed her own ulcerated leg by wrapping it in afterbirth when none of the prescribed pharmaceuticals worked. They said she kept afterbirth in a jar in the refrigerator right next to the jug of milk when she needed it for herself or anyone else. I have no memories of going for a snack in her refrigerator and mistakenly eating afterbirth. I was mostly too frightened to get up in the night even to go to the bathroom because of all of the faces I envisioned in the unpainted pine walls of her house. I was even more stunned that other members of our family confessed they saved their children's afterbirth, too. Our immediate family certainly hadn't done this, and I'm sure my mother would've said, "That's just like your daddy's people."

The wet nurse and afterbirth stories were simply too good not to include in a story. Once finished, I sent the story off simultaneously to several literary magazines. One editor in New Jersey wrote me and said, "I don't want to publish this. It's gross. I think you should rewrite it. I just don't think anyone is going to publish it." She ended up taking another piece I'd written, and in the next few days, I got an acceptance for the story from a literary magazine in Australia.

Difference doesn't always come from my own experience with family or friends. It's often relayed to me by others. A lady from a seminar I taught at a Methodist church came up to me and said, "I was at the doctor's office last week and I was listening to these two old women. One of them said to the other, 'Hell, it's been so long now, I don't even remember my first husband.' I laughed about that and kept telling myself I had to tell you about it. Maybe you can use it in one of your stories." When she told me, I laughed, too, and felt it was out of the ordinary and that I should definitely include it in the dialogue of a story.

Sometimes, it's not that the language or phrase is unique, but how it's conveyed. I once interviewed my maternal grandmother for a college social work project to determine patterns of family dysfunction. I asked her about alcoholism in our family and she gently assured me there were no alcoholics in our family. There was a pause and I felt relieved my project would be an easy one; however, she then added, "Now, we had family who used to drink a lot, but they weren't alcoholics."

She went on to tell me of her grandfather who owned a large farming operation and would get drunk, shoot up the house, and then go to town in his buggy the next day to buy his wife all new furniture. She talked about how he held a gun on his daughter, my great grandmother, and made her play the piano for him all night until he passed out, how she and the other grandchildren would run into the woods and hide all night for fear of being shot. She told me how he would get drunk and jump into the well and try to drown himself. When I asked if he'd died of cirrhosis, she said, "No, he and his nephew got drunk and shot each other to death in a duel over something none of us remember now." But, we had no history of alcoholism in our family. I remember being stunned by her stories, especially years later near the end of her life when she talked about how she had wanted to go to college and be a writer. In fact, she had written a book that had been thrown into the fireplace and burned, and she was told she would go to work on the farm to help until she got married.

My grandmother's stories were not all sad, though. One of my favorites was when she and her sister smoked marijuana for the first time in their mid-eighties while at the beach. They'd heard it would help their eyes and tried it. My grandmother said to her sister, "I don't feel a thing." She got up from her rocking chair on the porch of the beach house and fell flat on her face and began laughing. Then, her sister, said, "Honey, are you okay?" Then, she began laughing, too, and, for the next ten minutes, they just laughed. I never asked where they bought marijuana and couldn't believe they had drug connections. Another time, my mother had taken her for an eye doctor's appointment and her eyes were dilated. She wasn't able to drive, but she insisted she could and pulled out in front of a tractor-trailer that jack-knifed and landed in a ditch. She took off down the highway in her Mercury Marquis knocking down orange cones for miles that had been put out to protect the freshly painted lines. When my first collection *Road Kill Art and Other Oddities* was published, my grandmother was dying from cancer in the hospital. My mother read my grandmother the stories and I talked briefly with my grandmother by phone and told her that I'd made her famous to which she replied, "Where's my check?"

My writing does not always reveal family issues or eccentric anecdotes. I have adapted fictitious variations of historical stories that highlight difference. In my latest novel *Drifting Too Far from the Shore*, I used the ancient literary device known as story within a story (or nesting) to call attention to some rather brutal tragedies. In one, a lynch mob in southern Georgia murdered Mary Turner, a pregnant African American female, and her unborn fetus in the beginning of the twentieth century. After she made some remarks that were considered unacceptable by the community, the lynch mob took her to a nearby river, where she was hung upside down in a tree. Her belly was split open and her living fetus dropped to the ground, where they stomped it, poured gas on it and burned it. She, too, had her clothes burned off while hanging in the tree and being riddled with bullets. Another example was about Hispanic migrant workers who were murdered just a few years ago. Women were raped and men were beaten to death by drug-crazed thugs who knew that the migrant workers kept all their wages in cash and with them. The laws in place would not allow the migrant workers to have bank accounts. I also used a story about "butterfly people" who helped save children during a tornado. In most instances, the children were the only ones who saw what they described as butterfly people. Each of these stories is radically different from mainstream stories about angels. Having characters in the novel recount these "true stories" and weave them into the narrative of the outer story underscores their importance on a number of levels.

Illustrating difference in fiction functions in a perpendicular fashion from what we consider our reality—like a stop sign at a crossroads. As a result, we stop in our reading, our perception shifts and expands, and we learn and grow. While capturing difference elicits highly charged emotional moments of empathy or humor, more often than not, these are opposite sides of the same coin. If we don't somehow integrate the unique and different, we become stagnant. I am appreciative and more blessed than I will likely ever know to have my own misfit island of family, friends, and experiences that allow me the opportunity to capture the essence of difference in writing. Whether it's my dad giving away used Pizza Hut pans as wedding gifts, the lady at the cleaners giving me someone else's clothes and insisting they're mine, or seeing someone read a book while driving eighty miles per hour in eight lanes of traffic in Atlanta, I'll continue to capture difference in writing.

A Woman Explains How Learning Poetry Is Poetry and Not Magic Made Her a Poet

Jacqueline Allen Trimble

I am a poet. That statement elicits the most curious expressions from people. If I lead with, "I'm a college professor," the response is usually, "Oh [uttered with delight], what do you teach?" But the poet thing invites a very different kind of "Oh," one complicated by memories of impenetrable esoterica or clumsy doggerel written by Aunt Gertrude or Uncle Fred. Their eyes fill with pity and derision as they appraise me. I can see them thinking, "Funny, she doesn't look crazy," or "I wonder exactly how many cats she owns?" Invariably, somebody says, "I don't really like poetry. It's too hard to understand" or "Nobody reads poetry anymore." Because such encounters take place at cocktail parties or banquets, I do not have time to explain the state of poetry in the thirty seconds I will have before the listener spots a long-lost friend across the room and scurries off. If I did have time, I would say poetry was once the highest form of genius. It is very much alive. William Carlos Williams's red rain-glazed wheelbarrow remains beside the white chickens, Elizabeth Bishop's great fish is being let go at this very moment, and somewhere Toi Derricote's black boys are playing the classics in the subway. New poets are being born every day, challenging the old forms, carving out new possibilities, creating new interest and excitement. Where will the brilliance of Claudia Rankine, Tyehimba Jess, Nate Marshall, or Morgan Parker take us? What new audiences will they engender or old audiences will they inspire? On any given night in big cities and small towns poets lift their voices in words of social justice. They lay bare our darkest secrets and force us to talk about what we must if we are to survive together. Filmmakers are even making movies of poems. No, my friend, poetry is more alive than ever. Which is precisely why at a time in my life when I should be slouching toward retirement, I am still trying to become the poet I always imagined I would be.

It has taken me five decades to claim the title poet in earnest. I would not recommend anyone follow my path to the writing life. For the past thirty-two years, I have taught college students literature, theory, composition, how to analyze, how to break a text down to its specific components and how put it back together. I have even had a hand in bludgeoning a few poems to death for the sake of education. Mostly, I have pulled back the curtain and shown them how writers create meaning out of sound and line, how they use connotation to take us where they want us to go and images as mirrors to our deepest wishes. I have done my job and destroyed the illusion of writing as magic. Yet, I continue to feel woefully inadequate as a poet. I am full of self-doubt. Most writers I know feel this way. This uncertainty, this perpetual dissatisfaction is what keeps us writing.

HOW I BECAME A POET

In the summer of 1968, the same year my father died and Martin Luther King Jr. was assassinated, my mother and I took a long road trip to California. We went to visit her sister Harriet. I was seven and, as is often the way with children, completely oblivious to the polarized political world in which I lived. What trepidation my mother must have felt as she loaded up our car and we set off on that westward journey through Mississippi, Louisiana, the wide expanse of Texas, and beyond. I was the navigator. She taught me to read road signs, to follow the network of highways, to point our way, but I am sure she had already mapped the territory. How carefully she must have figured out where to stay, where to be settled when darkness fell—how to negotiate unpredictable terrain.

My mother's face rarely betrayed her. If she were frightened, a newly widowed black woman travelling alone with a girl child, she never showed it. For me, the delight of Holiday Inns, the adventure of milkshakes filled with dried dates, a landscape evolving from southern forest to desert was all that I could see. The world was a solid stack of weekday pancakes and little crackers in cellophane waiting for pats of real butter. For two thousand miles, I amused my mother with chatter and stories. Sometimes I read to her: *Little*

Lulu by the Seashore, a book I adored as much as she detested, or *A Child's Treasury of Poems*, the first poetry collection I ever owned. My mother could recite "Father William" with little prompting and other poems like "Baby Seed Song" she had read as a child. I learned from her the pleasure of memorization, the joy of owning the language of a poem and by repetition and practice its sound and meaning. Sometimes, we made up words. "Thotum" was the face we made when we ate grapefruit. "Ting-o-ling" was her name for me because she said my laugh sounded like a bell. And so we rode on, buoyed by the travel and a desire to leave our sadness behind us. By the time we reached Los Angeles and Aunt Harriet's bougainvillea-covered house with a real lemon tree in the backyard, Alabama was as far away psychically as it was geographically.

That same year, I began to write, pecking out my autobiography on my grandfather's old portable Royal typewriter. It was one paragraph. Was this a coincidence, the timing of this trip and the birth of my desire to write? Probably. It is more likely I began to write that year because I had learned to read in Mrs. Edna T. Moseley's class, or because I lived in a house filled with books, or because I had been mesmerized by the rhythms of the King James Bible in Sunday school. So many variables, genetic and environmental, known and hidden, conspired to make me a writer. But I like to think the expansion of my geographical boundaries broadened my imagination as well, and because this is my story, I will say that this trip took me out of my small Alabama city and inspired me toward a writing life.

The day I put that piece of paper in my grandfather's typewriter and discovered myself in words, I was guided by intuition, my mother's love of books, and a community that iterated the value of language again and again. As a child, I did not know any writers, had never met one, but I knew preachers who excited whole congregations with the rhythm of their prose. The women shouted and the men waved their hands or stood and clapped as God was manifested through words. In the afternoons, brilliant, dignified, articulate women put on their finest frocks and recited the poetry of Paul Laurence Dunbar and Langston Hughes at teas and socials held in the basement fellowship hall. Afterwards, there were little finger sandwiches, mints, nuts, bowls of lime frappé that were only served on special occasions. Poetry equaled all I knew of glamour. Soon, I would be reciting too. It was the custom of that time for children to memorize "pieces" and to perform them on programs. I preferred long poems like Eliot's "The Naming of Cats" and

Poe's "The Raven." Adults nodded and smiled with appreciation. "Doesn't she speak well," they would say, then wink at me. The afternoon a friend undercut my performance of "Macavity, the Mystery Cat" with her rendition of "When Malindy Sings" drew my pique and admiration. Poetry recitation could be brutal sport.

Around town, when grown folks gathered in living rooms to play Pokeno or Gin Rummy, they told stories and jokes until they rolled with laughter and could hardly see their cards. From the children's table, I marveled at the quickness of their wit, the sting and comradery of their well-turned quips. It was all that I could do not to join in with a line or two of my own. How I longed for their eyes and ears to turn to me as I told my own tale, as I earned their appreciation and evoked their joy. In beauty shops and barbershops, men and women solved the problems of the world. They could exegete the Bible, and then, turning their attention to more mundane matters, these self-taught philosophers could offer claim and evidence in a single rhetorical question: "With all he done, how come George Wallace is governor again, and I'm still a po' black man trying to make it?" Everywhere was the pleasure of words. In such a world where even corner-store butchers invent lines like, "You look like a girl who knows what to do with collard greens," what else could I do but dream of lonely garrets and berets?

So I wrote my way through childhood and adolescence. I read my way through library stacks and wrote some more until the word-rich days of my childhood faded under the weight of time, career, and domestic life. As my husband often reminded me, "Writers write." And for a long time, a very long time, I did not write. At least, I did not write poetry very often. Instead, I talked about being a writer, someday. Someday when my children were grown or I had tenure or I had learned to grow parsnips. While I was wait-ing, I taught other people how to write. I told myself, "I am a teacher. That is enough." But it was not enough. I knew it would never be enough every time an academic article suddenly turned into a poem or when every open mic found me sitting in the audience clutching a handful of verse. *Writers write.* What was I to do? I had neither the time nor the energy to create anything. I had laundry, two small children, and a dissertation to finish. There was no time for poetry.

What I forgot, temporarily, is that both Ecclesiastes and the Byrds got it right: "to everything there is a season." What is fortunate about being a writer is that season may come early or late. By the time I took up writing again, I was already more than a decade older than John Keats was when he died. It's a good thing too. While Keats got it done early, I am still plodding my way to my own bright star. At a point in my life when I had all but given up on the idea of being a poet, a curious thing happened. My husband and I went to hear Alice Walker read at a marvelous African American bookstore in Montgomery, Alabama, the now (unfortunately) defunct Roots and Wings. After the reading, my husband asked her, "What can I do to help my wife write?" Alice Walker said, "Do the dishes." The words hung above the audience's laughter and spread over me like a benediction. *Do the dishes.* As my mother used to say, "You know it but you don't believe it." For years I had taught people that learning to write was about reading, effort, practice, and repetition. I had made my students revise again and again. I had insisted they study and understand structures in the work of others and in their own work. There was much to be learned from each unsuccessful attempt. Yet, I had not listened to my own instruction. I was waiting for inspiration. Waiting for the leisure time and space to think great thoughts. Waiting. I had clung to the belief that writing was magic, a thing of inspiration, and not of intentionality and work.

Frankly, I want to blame William Wordsworth with his, "Poetry is the spontaneous overflow of powerful feelings: it takes its origin from emotion recollected in tranquility," for filling my head with these useless Romantic notions (273). Except, I cannot blame Wordsworth because he also writes, "our continued influxes of feeling are modified and directed by our thoughts" (265) as he explains how and for what purpose *Lyrical Ballads* was constructed. He is writing about craft in the face of an enormous paradigm shift of form and thought with the advent of what would be called Romanticism. Inspiration must be shaped by habits of mind. The blindness had been mine. *Do the dishes.* There would be no magical someday, no room of my own, no great gust of energy falling like manna from heaven. There did not have to be. Walker had made it plain. If I were going to be a poet, something else— dishes, television, parsnips—would have to go, and I would have to let it go to make room for poetry. A decade later, my husband, youngest son, and I loaded up the car and headed more than a thousand miles to Cape Cod and a writing workshop run by Marge Piercy. My writing life had at last begun again. This time with a journey north.

HOW I FOUND MY SUBJECT AND REEVALUATED MUCH OF WHAT I HAD BEEN TAUGHT ABOUT WRITING

Writing is an art that has been practiced for a very long time by many, many people much smarter than I am. Knowing this comforts me. It assures me that I or anyone else can become a better writer with intention, practice, and the help of our literary ancestors. Writing can be learned. One of my favorite writing teachers said unequivocally that he does not believe in talent. My first instinct was to balk at this notion. If there's no such thing as talent, how am I special? That question implies the problem. Many of us cling to the fantasy that the finger of God has imbued some of us with a magic gut fire, and if we just tap into it, brilliance will tumble out onto the page effortlessly like water from a metaphorical babbling brook. To be sure, there are a few geniuses among us. Very few. I am not a genius. Most writers are not geniuses, and most of those who appear to be have created that illusion by the steady, consistent application of enormous sweat equity. Letting go of the idea that I am special has allowed me to substitute something much more important for my imagined poetic soul: craft. Developing craft requires an understanding of the strategies by which poems are put together—lineation, music, repetition, order, and the rest. These things may only be learned by reading and writing, reading and writing, reading and writing. Once I began to learn strategy, I was able to give up the idea that subject matter makes the poem, a notion even more detrimental to writing poetry than the primacy of talent over work.

As a young writer, I was taught to love universality. Through this conduit, I could enter any poem, even one that bore no semblance to my life nor took up any crosses I was likely to bear. I was encouraged to disdain the political, to write about subjects with which all people could connect—love, death, time, cats and toads. There were other rules. Be careful of the racialized. This limits the audience. Don't take up causes—women's issues, gender issues, working-class issues. Do not rant about social justice. Poetry is poetry, not a treatise. If I were to be a writer, I would have to learn to write in a way that left my poetry unmarked by blackness or femaleness. Poets who chose otherness as their bailiwick risk not being published or pigeonholed or forgotten. I asked no questions, never thought once why I might be writing, never queried my teachers about June Jordan or Sonia Sanchez or Gwendolyn Brooks or Lucille Clifton. I barely knew these women existed. I was far too busy reading the assigned Eliot, Warren, Tate, and Frost. Why did it not occur to me to ask how "Sweeny Among the Nightingales" is universal and "Poem About my Rights" is merely political? I made myself as inconspicuous as possible in my poetry and tried to write allusion-filled verse, which addressed big philosophical questions and employed a distant, commanding authorial voice.

The problem was I produced poetry that was not very interesting to read, certainly not to me. The problem was I was writing about someone else's subjects. The problem was trying to write a universal poem was not working for me. And yes, we are all human. And yes, we are connected by that spark inside us that creates the empathy we often feel for one another. And yes, we all matter—theoretically—though history has shown us that some of us matter more than others. What I find far more interesting, however, is we are creatures of particularities: specific geographies, histories, positionalities, temperaments, cultural idiosyncrasies, and lives. Because we occupy differing positionalities that are often shaped by race, gender, and class, we do not experience the world in the same manner. As a writer, my angle of reflection is informed by events and contexts particular to me, and I write from that place of knowing that only I can occupy. Some readers will connect with that place, and some will not. The edict to "be universal, not political" suggests that all writing is not political and that there is a central human something that allows us to connect with all texts. Impossible. This sort of thinking has been used to erect a universality fortress guarded by sentries who arbitrate who is allowed in and who is not. Who are these sentries, and how did they come to rule the marketplace of ideas? Why do they get to decide whose story is universal, thus important, and whose story is not? Each poem is a production of a historical moment, cultural sensibility, and the writer's idiosyncratic mind. I spent years trying to write like x when I was not x. While the poets who came before us or who write alongside us are essential to our writing, their value lies in craft, not subject.

As a black, woman writer, most of what draws my attention has historically not been considered universal. I come from a long line of people who have raged against the myth of black inferiority. My aunt Mahala graduated from law school in the 1930s and practiced law in the state of Alabama during a time when few women and no black women were doing that. My mother was a civil rights activist, and I spent my childhood falling asleep in meetings during which people strategized for equality. To be a writer for me is an act of resistance. To be a poet is to distill that resistance expeditiously into line and sound. I have been admonished that political writing is too ephemeral, too of the moment. *Oh, Jackie, when black boys are no longer shot in the street, who will read that poem? When women are no longer in sexual peril, who will care? When there is social justice for everyone, what will these poems mean or matter?* As a writer who believes that poetry is useful, not just decorative, and that its best use is to give voice to the silenced, I say, if this poem has saved black boys from bullets, and women from danger, and oppressed people from oppression, if it need never be read again, good. Let love and butterflies be the subjects of the day. Until then, I write for social justice. My poems will come from the newspapers and the television and the streets. They will be born of rage.

HOW TO WRITE POEMS FROM THE NEWSPAPER, TELE-VISION REPORTS, AND THE STREETS

A friend of mine asked me, "How do you write rage without screaming or scaring people away?" This question is an interesting one and based on a number of assumptions. My friend erroneously equates rage with screaming. Rage is the level after screaming. It is quiet, the angry lava descending the mountain, incinerating everything in its path. I find Lucille Clifton's "won't you celebrate with me" to be filled with rage. Those final lines "come celebrate / with me that everyday / something has tried to kill me / and has failed" is both sweet invitation and indictment (Clifton 475). And yet, the political and historical underpinnings on which the rage floats are a function of fact, "born in Babylon / both nonwhite and woman" (475). These facts have put the speaker's life in danger of "something" that would kill her, but the impotence of that something in the face of her resistance to being defined by a measuring stick other than her own, "what did I see to be / except myself," has led her to celebrate survival and invite others to join (475).

Natasha Trethewey also employs this strategy of evoking rage by laying bare the facts, often with little commentary. For example, in "Miscegenation" she tells the story of her parents' interracial 1965 marriage, illegal in Mississippi, connecting it to the historical and literary South (slavery and Faulkner), her own naming while her father was reading *War and Peace*, and sin: "They crossed the river into Cincinnati, a city whose name / begins with a sound like *sin*, the sound of wrong—*mis* in Mississippi" (Trethewey 36). The repetition of "Mississippi" as the final word of each of the poem's seven couplets echoes the "mis," and puts the onus of the "sin" where it always belonged, on the state's actions and not the individuals who did nothing but marry and reproduce. The final words "it means *Christmas child*, even in Mississippi" suggests that there are truths that must be acknowledged everywhere (36). The quiet rage in the poem comes through ruthless juxtapositions and repetitions: Joe Christmas, the biracial protagonist who is shot and castrated in Faulkner's *Light in August*, is paired with Jesus, the real Christmas child, and the narrator, also biracial, whose name means Christmas; the idea of *War and Peace*, the Russian novel, is played against Mississippi itself, the illegality of interracial marriage, and the speaker whom it produces. The language of "mis," a prefix meaning "wrongly," repeats throughout the poem like a mantra as if the speaker is shouting "wrong, wrong, wrong," without shouting at all. These are strategies of craft.

The second part of the question that expresses the need not to frighten people assumes poetry's purpose is to comfort and not agitate. If that were all poetry was fit for, we should study greeting cards instead of Amiri Baraka. To my thinking, to scare or incite is the best use of poetry. I write and want to write poetry that beckons the reader in through humor and misdirection, and then makes the reader vibrate with discomfort. For example, in the poem/song "The Revolution Will Not Be Televised," Gil Scott-Heron uses commercial references and repetition to create a text as thick with humor as it is with rage. It rails against the distraction of consumerism at the same time it encourages socio-political activism. Much of its language comes straight out of advertising: "The revolution will not go better with Coke. / The revolution will not fight germs that may / cause bad breath" (Scott-Heron 285). I used this strategy of taking familiar, vernacular language routinely found in television commercials to undercut or expose the destructiveness of what we watch in my "Ethnophaulism for the News." It occurred to me that so much of what gets reported on the news suborns racism even though the language seems nonjudgmental, even egalitarian. Thinking about Scott-Heron's "The Revolution Will Not Be Televised," I decided to write a series of short sound bites using the style and language of typical newscasts, but replacing "African American" or other politically acceptable terms with racial epithets. Nothing else about the blurbs changed. For me it was a way to convey the rage many people feel at systemic racial inequality everywhere, even on the daily news, by exposing what is said even when it is not said.

In commenting on this poem, Douglas Green, a poet and professor, wrote, "'Ethnophaulism for the News' (you may have to look it up, as I did) will likely shock, annoy, anger, and hurt potential readers of almost every racial and ethnic background. . . . Yet I have read no literary work, other than Coates' epistolary essay and Rankine's prose lyric, that captures so wittily and at the same time so directly and starkly the racial crises of the current moment and the way they are playing out in the media" ("On 'The Coddling of the American Mind'"). The poem works because of its strategy, not its subject or even because it is saying something new. It is not, but form has a way of changing the angle of seeing, the way altering light intensity or the position of its source makes a room look different at varying hours of the day. We often see something new when it appears in a different light.

This new angle of reflection is often accomplished through lineation. A line is a moment of attention. If there are two words, ten words, one word on a line, it makes a difference, alters meaning. Grouping the lines adds another layer. If the poem is a series of couplets or quatrains or sestets, if it is long and skinny down the page or fat and squat—a dense verse paragraph—a stone in the center of a white landscape or a lacey thing, feather light, all of this plays into the strategy of how a poem evokes what it evokes. It is marvelous for writers, then, that the word processor exists. Words may be deleted, lines moved, whole paragraphs cut down and dragged into rightful place with the command of a finger. And whatever we do can just as easily be undone with a stroke. Why shouldn't we play? A poem, after all, is not a sacred object, a thing to be worshipped as it comes out of the mind. Every line, every word is subject to deletion or reassignment. I have redeployed whole verses into entirely new poems. To do this well, the writer must learn to be fearless and to see the poem with the cool, appraising eye of the sculptor. Sometimes a chisel is necessary. Sometimes a sledgehammer.

HOW BEING SOUTHERN, BLACK, AND A WOMAN COMPLICATE MY WRITING LIFE

When I was in graduate school, I stopped at a large, chain book store in Birmingham on my way to Tuscaloosa. A longtime literary snob, I prefer independent book stores staffed by people who read, can enter F-a-u-l-k-n-e-r without asking the spelling or his first name, and who have at least heard of James Baldwin. And so I entered with some slight trepidation in search of a few Toni Morrison novels, though I felt fairly confident that even this barren land of self-help books and lattés carried one of the most well-known and praised writers of our time. When fifteen minutes of searching the fiction section yielded no luck, I began to feel shaky. No books by the Nobel-Pulitzer-National Book Award goddess? Not possible. And yet, there was not a single one of her novels in the fiction section. Nothing to do but ask a salesclerk and pray for a logical answer or at least that he had heard of her.

"Pardon, me," I said. "I can't seem to find any Toni Morrison novels in the fiction section."

"Oh, no. You won't find them there," he said, motioning toward another part of the store. "We keep them in the southern section."

Pause. "The southern section?" I stammered. "But Morrison is from Ohio." Even this chain store must realize that.

"I know," the clerk said cheerily, "but people think she's a southern writer, so we put her in the southern section. You know. So people can find her."

Oddly enough, I understood this strange logic. I, too, was drawn to the "southernness" in her writing. A few years later I would return to Birmingham, Alabama, to hear Toni Morrison deliver a lecture in which she talked about her mother, who was from Alabama, her father, who was from Georgia, and their migration from the Deep South to Ohio like many of their generation. *There it is*, I thought. *There is the southern sensibility that anchors her work.*

But here's the thing: there is no monolithic South. I live in a place where contradictions reside side by side. The Southern Poverty Law Center sits on the same street as the First White House of the Confederacy. One block over on Dexter Avenue, the nineteenth-century Capitol City Guard, an all-black regiment of which my husband's great-grandfather was the captain, marched, slaves were auctioned, Martin Luther King Jr. sat in his office strategizing for equality, and Jefferson Davis took his oath of office. In this same city the order was sent to fire on Fort Sumter, starting the Civil War, and Equal Justice Initiative (EJI) will build a memorial to people who were lynched under a corrupt, oppressive system. This odd little blip in the universe happens to be my home. What better place to write from than a place of epic contradictions?

A professor once said to me, "Southerners don't transplant well." He was right. I lived outside the South for two years and hated every minute of it. I did not understand the people, the customs, the food, or the accents. I wrote pastoral after pastoral as I longed for the sound of home. When I reentered Alabama after that long absence, I stopped my car, got out and kissed the ground. Even the kinship I feel to Morrison's work springs from my own sense of what it means to be black, a woman, and southern, complicated identities often at odds with each other, and sometimes at war. What does it mean to write the world from such a conflicted vantage point? As W. B. Yeats said, "Out of the quarrel with others we make rhetoric; out of the quarrel with ourselves we make poetry." My poetry comes out of my quarrel with myself as I grapple with the dualities of my feelings about the South, my home, my lovely, dysfunctional home—pride and shame; joy and sadness—the place from which comes both the love and rage that undergird my work.

WORKS CITED

Clifton, L. (2012). "won't you celebrate with me." In K. Young, and M. S. Glaser, eds., *The Collected Poems of Lucille Clifton 1965-2010* (427). Rochester, NY: BOA Editions, Ltd.

Green, D. (2015, September 18). "On 'The Coddling of the American Mind.'" Retrieved January 31, 2017, from academia.edu.

Scott-Heron, G. (2014). "The Revolution Will Not Be Televised." In John H. Bracey Jr., Sonia Sanchez, and James Smethurst, eds., *SOS—Calling All Black People: A Black Arts Movement Reader* (283). Amherst: University of Massachusetts Press.

Trethewey, N. (2006). *Native Guard*. Boston: Houghton Mifflin.

Wordsworth, W. (2006). Preface to *Lyrical Ballads* (1802). In M. H. Abrams et al.eds., *The Norton Anthology of English Literature, Eighth Edition* (263-74). New York: W. W. Norton.

VI

A Little Help from My Friends

Honey, it isn't the way I would do it, but you go right ahead.
—WILLIAM FAULKNER, RESPONDING TO A REQUEST BY HIS FRIEND EUDORA
WELTY FOR CRITICISM OF A LOVE SCENE SHE HAD WRITTEN.

Hard Labor:
The Birth of a Novelist

Susan Cushman

*I*n October 2006 I met five women who would unwittingly become instigators in the long, laborious process of my birthing as a novelist. Lee Smith, Cassandra King, Beth Ann Fennelly, Jennifer Horne, and Wendy Reed (most of whom have essays in this collection) were speaking at the Southern Festival of Books the last year the festival was hosted by Memphis. (Nashville has hosted the annual event since then.) Lee was giving a talk about her latest book *On Agate Hill*, and I instantly became a fan. Although we didn't have much time to talk personally, I was drawn to her voice, and I was inspired by her longevity—she had written and published ten novels over a period of forty years. Beth Ann had a nonfiction book out, *Great with Child*, but I was mesmerized by her poetry collection, *Tender Hooks*, and like most people when they first meet Beth Ann, I had a huge girl crush. She had on snug jeans with tall boots, and her beautiful auburn hair hung halfway down her back in sexy waves. Jennifer and Wendy were on a panel discussing an anthology they co-edited, *About Faith: Southern Women on Spirituality*, which made me want to run home and pen an essay immediately. But my most vivid memory from the weekend is a conversation I had with Cassandra as she signed a copy of her latest novel, *The Sunday Wife*. Our stories were similar, in that we both were married to ministers and spent years doing the "expected thing" with our art—creating religious pieces for the church newsletter or bulletin and writing children's Christmas plays. It wasn't until she shared her Truth (capital T intentional) with me—that she had always wanted to write novels—that we embraced, and she signed my copy of her book, "To Susan, who knows what a Sunday Wife is." A seed was planted, and hope was springing up in me. Could I become a novelist? I fell in love with each of these women for different reasons, but they all inspired me, as did the novelist Joshilyn Jackson, whom I had met the previous summer at the first annual Mississippi Writers Guild Conference. Best-selling short story author John Floyd critiqued my less-than-wonderful attempt at writing short fiction, and I knew then I needed the longer narrative form to tell a decent story. Since I'm originally from Jackson, Mississippi, it was a joy to share a weekend with established and up-and-coming writers from my home state, and I found myself singing along with Rodney Atkins's song "These Are My People" on the radio as I drove back to Memphis.

Over the next few months I wrote my first novel, *The Sweet Carolines*, in a coffeeshop. It remains in a box on a shelf, but some of its characters and plotlines emerged as incarnations in my later work. Struggling with fiction, I took to writing essays and was happy to find publishing homes for a dozen or more of them over the next ten years. As Anne Lamott says, the essay is so much easier to write than the novel—it's more like a one-night stand, whereas writing a novel is more like a marriage. But since I've been married forty-seven years, I should have acquired the patience and perseverance to write a book-length story, right?

Next I tried my hand at memoir, as much for therapy as art. But eventually I realized that I wasn't willing to go public with some of the names that peopled my stories of childhood and young adulthood sexual abuse and unhappiness in the cult-like religious group in which I spent almost two decades of my life. One of my mentors, the author Scott Morris, critiqued my early chapters of the memoir at the Yoknapatawpha Summer Writers Workshops (a.k.a. the YOK Shop) I attended in Oxford, Mississippi, several summers between 2007 and 2015. He taught me that if I was going to write "confessional prose," I needed to learn to get up and above the pain and make *art*. It was then that I realized I should try fiction again.

In 2010 and 2011, I drafted a new novel, *Cherry Bomb*. Scott and my fellow participants at the YOK Shop critiqued early drafts of *Cherry Bomb*, and the first three chapters made the short list in the "Novel-in-Progress" category of the 2011 Faulkner-Wisdom Creative Writing Competition. In 2012 I hired a freelance editor and enlisted several "early readers"—and the members of the writing group I was in at the time—to give feedback on the manuscript and help me polish the book. Next I spent six months querying seventy-five literary agents. About twenty-five of them asked to read the full manuscript, and many wrote really nice rejection letters. Finally agent number seventy-five *loved* the book. She asked if she could send it to an editor for an overview (at a cost of $750) and I didn't know any better than to say yes.

For the next two years (with a three-month interruption when I was in a car wreck and couldn't work) I worked with this agent, even meeting with her in person in New York City, and she continued to tell me she loved the book. But she also continued to convince me to send it to yet another editor (for another $750) as it wasn't quite "up to commercial standards" yet. This process was extremely frustrating, as these editors often gave me contradictory advice. The book has three main characters. One editor encouraged me to completely delete one of the characters (and the three chapters written in her voice) while another editor declared that character to be her favorite in the book. One editor encouraged me to read *The Girl with the Dragon Tattoo* and to make my protagonist more "hard ass"—like Lisbeth Salander—while another asked me to rewrite the entire manuscript, changing it from present tense to past tense. As I shared my struggles with several friends who were published authors, each of them expressed concerns about the agent charging me for editing. When she asked me if she could send it out for a fourth major revision, I parted ways with her. That was one of the hardest things I have ever done.

I spent the next few months querying agents again, and after another fifty (yes) rejections, I finally made the decision to give up on my dream for a book deal with one of the big publishing houses. I began querying small presses that don't require agent representation, and finally, in November 2016, I signed a contract with a small press in Mississippi. *Cherry Bomb*—a novel about a graffiti writer, an abstract expressionist painter, and a nun, set mostly in Georgia—had found a home and would be published in August 2017. The editing process was so much better this time. Collaborating with the publisher, going through the manuscript chapter by chapter, we partnered to kill a few darlings and to birth a few more, lifting the narrative arc in places where it sagged and inserting scenes where more were needed. Working with a small press gave me a sense of ownership in my work. I was even invited to give input on the cover design, which was important to me as an artist. What I gave up (money? fame?) by not having an agent and a book deal with one of the big five, I gained in the joy of intimate involvement in every step of the publishing process.

So, in a sense, the birthing of my first novel was a ten-year labor of love. Along the way I often wondered if I have what it takes to be a novelist. I took some "detours," writing and publishing a nonfiction book about caregiving for my mother, who died of Alzheimer's in May 2016. *Tangles and Plaques: A Mother and Daughter Face Alzheimer's* was culled from sixty blog posts covering over eight years of Mother's decline. Back at that Mississippi Writers Guild Conference in 2006, Joshilyn had encouraged me to start a blog in order to build a platform and grow an audience of readers. Little did I know then that a decade later (posting religiously three times a week about topics like mental health, art, religion, writing, and literature) sixty of those posts would find new life as essays in a book.

Other detours included contributing essays to three anthologies. In all three cases, my experience working with the editors of these anthologies was positive. I came to realize how much I loved the genre, and decided to try and edit one myself.

A Second Blooming: Becoming the Women We Are Meant to Be was my first collection to organize and edit. I was through-the-roof with excitement as twenty excellent writers agreed to contribute (I even got a foreword by Anne Lamott), and Mercer University Press offered to publish the book. I began to think that I enjoy editing more than writing. And I've always loved to organize things—like the literary salons I host in our home here in Memphis several times a year—so grouping the essays by themes and finding quotes to anchor each section was simply fun. It was such a nice break from the labor-intensive writing and revising involved with the novel. I was so exhausted from the six years involved in the production of *Cherry Bomb* that I declared (as I'm sure many mothers have done postpartum) never to write another novel. But—also like those new mothers—it wasn't long before my mind began to long for another child and to dream up new characters and new locations and new plotlines. By the time this collection goes to press, I hope to have another novel in the oven. Yes, the pain of childbirth passes, and the possibility of bringing something literary, something hopefully wonderful, into the world is great enough to endure another pregnancy. In a sense, this essay is a thank-you letter to my early lovers—the ones who planted those first seeds—because I truly believe I would not have become a writer without them. But it's also a nod to future midwives whom I look forward to working with as the labor continues.

Lyrical Acts*

Wendy Reed

ACT I—LYRICAL BEDS (CIRCA 1970)

*M*y father used cinder blocks to grow tomatoes. It wasn't pretty but it worked. The whitish-gray hunks of masonry are functional, not decorative, and made when a Krispy Kreme–style conveyor belt funnels concrete into standard rectangular molds. Flat sides form around a pair of 6 × 6 holes that keep the weight at 28 pounds. Today one costs about $1.50, but I suspect Daddy didn't pay a dime, though he did buy the garden soil by the bag. He filled each hole with a small mountain of fresh dirt and poked a tomato plant into the pinnacle, a tiny green flag. Raised beds, then, were not a sign of urban chic or eating local. In fact, they were not a sign of anything, except hard soil that didn't drain.

Back then serious farmers plowed their acreage into long rows with tractors, and people like my father—"who decided to have a garden again this year"—dug narrow furrows into the dirt by hand, using a tiller. In only the smallest of small plots could you get by with a shovel.

On farms and in gardens, growing things was a matter of digging, because the dirt was already there. You might add fertilizer or water if it hadn't rained, but no one in their right mind covered up the dirt with more dirt.

Our backyard, though, had survived the trampling of three generations playing chase and freeze tag, and could no longer, according to Daddy, grow a decent tomato. The plants would bloom but their roots could barely tread water in the densely packed ground. They were not fit to eat solo or to grace a piece of Wonder Bread. The concrete kept the dirt elevated and in place, so the young roots could breathe and stretch downward, while above, the leaves worked their photosynthetic magic. The blocks gave the young seedlings a healthier foundation and each got off to a better start. By the time the roots hit stagnant ground, most had grown strong enough to thrive.

Thus I first learned about deliberate cultivation from unsightly raised beds.

⌖

Mother wanted a bigger bed, king- or queen-sized, but those cost money. So Daddy shoved my sisters' old twin beds together and pushed them against the wall, which he'd built. He'd built the whole house after they married. He'd been 19; she 14 1/2. Despite age, or should I say lack thereof, marriage will thrust a couple headlong into adulthood and its expectations. And a husband might, in order to put a roof over his bride's head, live with her parents while building it right next door.

Daddy could never understand why Mother wasn't happy with the walls as they were and why she was always wanting to hang one more thing. Having been born during the era of the Great Depression, my parents each had stories of struggle, but their versions were not the same. Hard work had always been a part of their lives along with everyone they knew, but for Daddy's family, it had not always been enough. He knew fields and want in a way Mother never would, so a roof and food on the table were goal enough for him. He did not need something else to go on a perfectly good wall. Sometimes it caused an argument but always it ended with hammering and a nail. Then came the ultimate hanging request, one that would completely cover up the sheetrock: paneling. By then they were grandparents and the once-and-oft contemplated divorce was no longer an option. In other words, they'd put it to bed, which may or may not have had something to do with mother wanting a bigger one.

Beds today are no longer bequeathed as they were in past centuries, when possession of beds—not unlike land in the South—designated status; they were valued by farmers alongside beasts of burden and slaves. In a Georgia will dated December 30, 1775, James Cunningham bequeathed to his daughter Ann "two slaves, a Saddle and Bridle now in her Possession, Ten Pounds Cash, two Cows and Calves, and a Bed."

Industrialization brought beds of mass production, so it wasn't availability that was an issue for Mother and Daddy. She could window-shop to her heart's content but to take one home required reckoning with the price tag.

Shift-work and layoffs breed a particular kind of frugality, more like getting by than half-assing it. It's a life art I once suggested in graduate school, in an attempt to wed blue-collar creativity with film criticism and launch a new theory I proposed be called Making Do. My professor covered the paper in incredulous red ink, and I barely got by with a B minus.

But Mother got her bigger bed, or at least a facsimile. They laid a new mattress on top of the twin beds and the pair of box springs and when she made it up using new sheets and one of Bigmama's quilts, she adjusted the bedspread so it hung to the floor and it did not look fake or like some sort of Siamese conjoined contraption. It looked genuine, like a real king-sized bed.

Kings and royals were the first to have their own beds. For everyone else beds were communal. Before chimneys came along, open hearths burned in the center of the room, and people slept on straw-filled mats on the floor because smoke does not sink, it rises. After the advent of chimneys and the air was clear, beds rose up off the floor.

In my first memory of my parents' new bed, I sit beside Mother. I must've been about three or four, because I haven't started school and can't yet read or write. Everything is quiet, no TV or telephone, so Daddy must've been working the 3-to-11 shift.

Mother never read me bedtime stories, but she would prop a pillow against the double cherry headboard and read silently to herself. Maybe that night it was *Love's Lost Stallion*, which, I'm guessing, was not about a horse. Whatever it was about, I knew all those words held Mother under some kind of spell.

What're you reading, Mother? Why? What's that word, Mother? What's it mean? What about that one, Mother? And that one? Mother? Mother?

At some point Mother shoved an old paperback at me. She had to have wanted to shove it into my mouth but instead she put it in my lap. I opened it and stared into the mystery for a while. It didn't take long until I started to fidget.

Mother?

Before I could say another word, she handed me a pen.

I can write in it? I asked.

Without looking up, she nodded.

I ran that pen all over those pages, long lines of swirls and curlicues like I'd seen adults and my cousin, who was a few years older than me, do. She'd graduated from "printing like babies do" to "real writing."

I would not learn the word *cursive* until second grade, but I knew everything went up and down and almost all the way to the end of the paper, but I did not let the margins stop me. Like some kind of EKG gone wild, I scribbled until my hand gave out.

I wonder what I thought I was writing.

Maybe this is why I don't think of myself as a real writer. Truth is, I can barely even type, but, man, can I scribble.

"The process of seduction starts once we learn as children that written words unlock a secret world. Literary seductions begin not with content of writing or its context, but at the level of the single black mark on a sheet of white paper," writes Frances Wilson in *Literary Seductions*. Nabokov, she reminds us, suggests, "one should notice and fondle details." In that case, I suspect he might've approved of Mother's *Lost Stallion*.

Before we decode an alphabet, Wilson says, "we respond to its letters and patterns much as a fetishist responds to the bit-parts of the body."

When I started school, I took to reading like nobody's business and Mother took to hiding her paperbacks. Eventually she bought me my own set of Britannica Jr. encyclopedias and went to work at the mall selling lingerie. (There's nothing worse than being fitted for your first bra by your mother.) With a full-time job, she quit reading. "I don't have the time anymore," she said.

According to Wilson, the French literary philosopher Roland Barthes compares reading "to those other solitary acts, praying and masturbation."

Mother didn't take me to church. It was up the street so I walked myself. She did, however, take me to the library to check out books.

Even so, I found those paperbacks.

ACT II—LYRICAL SEDUCTIONS
(CIRCA MY 50TH BIRTHDAY)

For Mother's 50th birthday, I threw her a surprise party. It was small—Daddy, my boyfriend, a couple of neighbors, her friend the belly dancer. Daddy's gift hung in her ears not on the wall, but because they had diamonds, she forgave him. As my 50th approached, my husband panicked. Parties, he will admit, give him hives. But the invitation I received from an old flame to spread his brother's ashes in the old neighborhood did not even give him pause.

"You don't mind?" I asked.

"Not if that's what you want to do."

Mr. Flame, as I'll call him, was an author whose books hadn't just been published, they'd been *translated*. Whatever that meant, it sounded impressive. I'd wanted to try my hand at a children's book, so I had called the local university to ask about a class and was told Mr. Flame would give me a call. A couple days passed. No call. So I called back and left another message. Still I didn't get a call, so I called back a third time.

"He's not in. May I take a message?"

"Does he work there or not?" I asked.

"He teaches class this evening. It might be best to try in person."

I arrived 20 minutes early. He was 20 minutes late. Let's just say we didn't get off to a good start.

But I took his class anyway and it turns out he took my scribbling seriously. He wrote comments on my stories as if they were real rather than made up and even claimed my second story was good.

I shrugged it off as beginner's luck and signed up for another class. At some point, he explained Southern Gothic to me and said I ought to consider writing country songs. While I pretended to understand the difference between southern and Southern Gothic, it seemed to me that they were the same thing, like July and August are both summer, but their heat radiates in varying degrees.

Still, I read every one of his comments a thousand times. And sometimes even more. They not only quenched a thirst I didn't know I had, they made me drunk with something I couldn't explain.

When I'd sober up, I'd tell myself he was just being nice, that he couldn't have meant them because deep down I knew I did not write, I read. For Pete's sake, I was a homonym: Wendy *Reed*. My last name was one loop away from read. But I was not a writer.

When his interest expanded beyond those comments, I felt confused. A note in my box at school. A letter under the writing lab door. My daughter coming in from the mailbox waving a postcard, "Someone forgot to put their name." Was he interested in me or my writing?

Maybe if I'd considered myself a writer, the answer wouldn't have seemed so clear.

Maybe if I'd heard of a literary seduction, a relationship where the reader first falls for the writing, I would have responded differently.

In Antonio Skármeta's novella *Il Postino*, the Chilean poet Pablo Neruda provides metaphors for the postman to woo a barmaid. Her mother is not amused. "With these metaphors, Don Pablo, he's got my daughter hot as a pistol. . . . We are in the thick of a very dangerous situation." She warns her daughter: "All men who first touch with words go much further afterwards with their hands. . . . There isn't a drug in the world worse than all that blah-blah-blah. It makes a village innkeeper feel like a Venetian princess. Later, when the moment of truth arrives, when life catches up with you, you'll realize that these words are no better than a bad check. I would much rather have a drunkard in the bar grab your ass than have someone tell you that your smile flies higher than a butterfly."

Mr. Flame wrote me from New York, where he'd traveled to see his work performed on stage. (I'd grown up thinking travel had to involve birthdays, funerals, or Panama City.) He'd also seen Nicole Kidman in an ad on the side of a bus. You remind me of her, he wrote, saying there was a glowing resemblance.

I should say here I'm an olive-skinned brunette with eyes the color of a black hole. But as I read his words again, I could suddenly see myself in the porcelain-faced, blue-eyed, redheaded star, and was surprised I hadn't noticed it before. In fact, she and I were probably twins.

Neruda told the postman: "You don't read the words—you swallow them. . . . You have to let them melt in your mouth."

Casanova, history tells us, did more than seduce with writing, though it's his bedding of 122 women (his count) that led to his reputation as a notorious cad. The literary and mathematical genius would be thrilled to learn that the Bibliothèque nationale de France in Paris recently purchased his twelve-volume *Histoire de ma vie* for $9 million. And those dozen volumes are just a fraction of the written work he left behind.

⚬

In *Literary Seductions*, Wilson suggests that all writing strives to seduce. It sets out to ensnare and captivate the reader, make her forget, if but for a moment, the world beyond print. Writing desires to be desired.

What, Wilson wonders, is going on between the writer and the writing and the reader and the reading that effects such a powerful attraction?

I now wonder, too.

⚬

My first love letter came from Mickey Crawford, the son of Mother's belly-dancing friend. We were in first grade. Mickey knocked at my front door with candy and an envelope and it wasn't even Valentine's Day. I recall hesitating but when I saw my name on the envelope, I invited him right in. The next note d'amour was an invitation from Keith Branham to skate during Couples Only, the moment at the roller rink when the lights go down, the mirrored ball begins to spin, and "Dream Weaver" or "Wildfire" starts to play over the PA system. A boy and girl—the only acceptable coupling in 1970s Birmingham—basically attempt to ballroom dance on eight wheels. Mostly, though, we all knew it was an excuse to touch. And an excuse for the boys to show off since skating backward took infinitely more skill than rolling forward. Keith and I were not even halfway around the floor before we switched places. Better I do the backward skating than we both wind up in casts. Next it was Kevin Real who wrote pages and pages proclaiming that I was his Holy Grail. He was *older*, and to my sixth grade, brace-face, four-eyed self an eighth grader represented the pinnacle of sophistication. He didn't need an excuse to hold my hand and closed his letters with "Je t'aime." Never mind that foreign languages wouldn't be an elective until high school, I just knew he was fluent. And every time I read them—and I read them a lot—they took on a thicker French accent until finally it sounded like I'd fallen for Pepé Le Pew.

Though I expected Mr. Flame to burn out, he stayed hot. I turned the relationship over in my mind every which way I could and looked at it from all the possible angles: student/professor; May/December; midlife crisis; finding myself; losing myself.

But they were all cliches.

Real writing abhors a cliche.

It was more than friendship or fling, but at some point I quit trying to name it and just let go. It is what it is, we said.

I think in retrospect, what I'd wanted was a mentor because though I could not say it then, I wanted to write my own metaphors, not be seduced by them. But seduction is never a one-way street. And for reasons I may never understand, the written word does "it" for me. Books, letters, emails, notes, even billboards, where I learned to recognize and read my first words—*Stuckey's 10 miles, Stuckey's 5 miles, Stuckey's 1 mile*—stir something in me I cannot resist. And while the written word may turn me inside out and upside down, it never ceases to turn me on.

You can have your oysters; give me the alphabet.

⌀

"I know you'll be busy because that's your birthday week," Mr. Flame said on the phone when I called to say I'd join him. "But I can fly in any day. What's good for you?"

We picked Sunday morning and because he wanted to scatter the ashes at several places, he volunteered to drive.

"Where should I meet you?"

"I'm not making this up; I swear he said, "The library.""

ACT III—WHAT THE HELL IS A LYRICAL, ANYWAY?

For one southerner to call another southerner crazy is redundant. But allowable. Just don't nobody else try it.

Carl Carmer snuck down south into Alabama by train nearly 100 years ago for a six-year stint as an English professor. It took a while but he learned to fit in. When he left, he wrote a book about the experience that pissed a lot of people off, but not because he got the stories wrong. He actually nailed them and *Stars Fell on Alabama* became a best-seller. Truth, you see, is rarely our issue. But Carmer had broken an unspoken rule. He wasn't from around here. He didn't have a right to tell our stories because they weren't his to tell.

"Crazy" is also a melodious song about heartbreak that Patsy Cline didn't want to record because she didn't like it. Who was this Willie Nelson writer anyway? During the first recording session, she was on crutches and couldn't hit the notes because of a broken rib. But in the second session, she did Nelson's song proud. It went to Number 2 on the charts and remains a classic as well as the title of a hit musical. The song sparked a much-desired comeback, and a year and a half later in May 1963, it and "I Fall to Pieces" concluded a benefit concert and her last-ever performance. While flying home, her plane crashed 90 miles outside of Nashville in a Camden forest off Firetower Road. Her recovered wristwatch had stopped at 6:20 pm.

It had been twenty years since that first class, and Mr. Flame had been contemplating his own mortality of late. As he drove past where our siblings had gone to high school, the hospital where we'd been born, the elementary school he'd attended—and I, because of city politics, missed attending by a year—I kept reminding myself it was his brother's life we were celebrating. I had been careful to stay in a specific lane of memory—childhood geography and siblings—things we had in common but had not shared.

We passed his childhood house and his teenage house and then headed to the house his parents had bought when he was in college. At some point his brother served in the armed forces and had returned changed. There were medicines and diagnoses, but as with my family, little was openly discussed and most swept under the nearest rug. With nowhere else to go, memories embed into our foundations and take on odd shapes.

Mr. Flame pulled into a 7-11 and parked. "They're in the trunk," he said. "They" being the cremains.

Once back in the car, he took a dark box out of a wine-colored velvet bag.

"You know they have to go through security with your shoes and belt."

I did not know. But I took his word for it.

He tried to open the box but it wouldn't budge. "They made it look easy when they showed me how."

I'd never seen him wear anything that wasn't wrinkled but today his white button-down looked like it had been ironed. I looked at my thighs. Twenty years can change a person. Instead of black tennis shoes like he'd always worn, he had on Keens. I was wearing Keens, too.

The weft of crazy is always there; it just doesn't always show. But it always makes a good story.

"Do you remember the kitchen?" he asked, pointing at the last house his brother had lived in.

I froze. He wasn't supposed to switch lanes of memory. I'd thought there was a tacit understanding. Today was not to discuss our history. My heart had healed. It'd been hard but Gloria was right. I survived. I had closure. No need to go back.

But then I thought, maybe he wanted to apologize.

"Vaguely," I said, giving my memory more time to dig. Nothing was coming up, though.

"You don't remember, do you?"

I wanted him to quit reading my face. Apparently some things after twenty years stay the same.

I tried harder but nothing appeared in my mind's eye except a fuzzy image that wouldn't come into focus. I don't know if I saw disgust or sadness on his face first, but the hurt was undeniable. Maybe it wasn't forgiveness but permission he was wanting. Maybe he wanted to write our story and had imagined this would provide the conclusion. That there'd be a poignant moment when we shared this memory, and that would be that.

Only I'd forgotten my part.

Time after time, I've been undone by what someone wrote to me. I've lived the push and pull of reading, and reading between the lines. I've pored over each syllable as if mining for gold, rereading the sentences once again to massage their meaning, to squeeze them just right until they yield beneath the pressure.

Writing is the intersection of action and deliberation, the axis where movement and stillness collide, it's the physicality of mentality, it's how we see the unseen.

To write is to combine the soul with pencil lead. Offer a map of your heart and mind and sigmoid colon. It's like hiking up your skirt.

It's transgressive, a way to sanction trespass. A ticket to the botanical garden of knowledge, a seat in the den of iniquity. It's peeling the forbidden fruit with a nib. It's not biting the apple but chewing as long as it takes.

It is squiggles and lines and angles, a geometric alchemy.

I like to think of Eve's apple as the first literary seduction, the first use of words to share something so delicious it will alter everything to come, and nothing will ever taste the same.

In his introduction to the *Best American Essays of 2016*, Jonathan Franzen says, "Risk is implicit from the minute you decide to write an essay rather than something casual, fragmentary, impromptu. The sheer act of carefully crafting a story raises the stakes."

Franzen is not southern. He can only understand risk on a cerebral level. A quick Googling reveals that of the twenty-three essays he chose, only one author is indisputably southern (according to a readily available survey of southerners that considers only four states to be really southern). But when you're southern, you have a reputation to uphold. Risk is just one small part of being crazy.

Carl Carmer claimed that in this exotic place called the South, "any unusual stimulus provokes an inevitable reaction to do something about it, something physical and violent."

Although we bitched so about his book, we started the next century by making sure its title was seen all over the state. Every car from 2002–2009 sported it because it was at the top of our license plates: STARS FELL ON ALABAMA.

Writing is not, however, a southern act. Frying stuff is. Putting gravy on our fluvastatin is. Tanning in a salon before going to the beach is. Writing is the act of making words flesh.

If Franzen is right, that writing an essay doesn't have to make sense, it just has to risk, then southerners are born for it. We expect our last words to be, "Hey watch this!"

◦

Flame and I spread ashes around town; most of the places were legal. All that spreading and traversing memory lane works up an appetite, so we stopped at Post Office Pies, but I ordered salad because I'm watching my carbs. Our conversation took a hard turn away from his brother and I began to wonder if the memorial was a ruse for something else. I was happily married and though he and his ex-wife had moved away from Alabama, they lived in the same city and "shared grandkid care and a mailbox." Maybe he wanted permission to write about us, or the "us" that almost was. We could've had something special; our love could've been a real contender. And those always make the best stories because the love never wears out. That's the thing about desire. Quench it and it's gone. But let it burn in our imaginations with a Heathcliff-ian "What if?" and it never has to die.

"I'm an old man," he said. "I haven't got much time." He paused and for the first time caught my eyes and held them. "We were happy, weren't we?" he asked.

I couldn't think what to say so I took a bite of arugula. He followed suit and stuck his fork into the enormous bed of greens spread before him. He didn't even pretend to like it.

"What is this?" he asked.

"Kale," I said.

After getting a mouthful down, he pushed the plate away. "Do you think we could stay in touch?"

"So this wasn't about your brother?" I asked. No need, I decided, to beat around the bush.

He did not answer but his eyes said everything I needed to know.

But unlike the first time he'd sat across from me and asked to spend some time with me, I was 50 now. Arugula notwithstanding, my salad days were over.

"Surely you knew?" he said.

But I don't think I did. If anything, I thought it might be a chance for him to apologize.

"I brought something," he said, then several typed pages appeared where his salad had been. "It was part of a book I wrote that the editor made me cut. I found it cleaning out my office and would like to read it to you, if that'd be okay."

What was I supposed to say?

To be fair, he never promised his students that he'd teach them to write. "I can tell you what I do but I can't write for you. And I'll tell you what someone once told me: 'You can live in my house until you get your own, but when you leave, burn it down.'"

The house of writing was not the bed of roses I'd imagined. I would never be Flannery O'Connor or Eudora Welty no matter how hard I tried. But maybe, just maybe, scribbling down all my life's stories, as odd as they are, is enough, even though it's not the type of literary real writing I'd envisioned. Not all songs, I suppose, are poetic after all. And though I should prefer anything by Pavarotti to Lynyrd Skynyrd, nothing sounds as right as "Sweet Home Alabama." Maybe enthusiasm counted more than I realized.

Maybe it was time to write that country song.

Maybe that song starts with Juliet beside her old flame in a red rental car, a box wedged between her knees. He can't get it open with his fingers so she pries it apart with her car key. And as she unbuckles her safety belt and opens the passenger door, she tries not to spill his brother.

* Without Frances Wilson's *Literary Seductions: Compulsive Writers and Diverted Readers*, this essay would not exist. I consider myself a quilter not a plagiarist, but if I missed an attribution, I do not mean to pass off her cloth as mine.

The Necessity of Writer Friends

Nicole Seitz

Friendship . . . is born at the moment when one man says to another,
"What? You too? I thought that no one but myself. . . ."
—C. S. LEWIS, *THE FOUR LOVES*

After years of working in corporate cubicles, one day I had an epiphany sitting at my desk on the second floor of my home. No coworkers were around save for the tiny one growing in my belly, a pre-diabetic cat named Espresso, and a three-and-a-half-pound Chihuahua, Kahlua, at my feet. Unshowered with messy hair, pajamas on and hot coffee in hand, I smiled and said a silent prayer of gratitude. *Lord, thank you for understanding me. For giving me peace.* No stress, no strife or bosses or meetings that used to suck up precious time. I was the boss now. *Ahhh, this is living,* I thought. With my computer screen and email as a shield, I no longer had to have human contact except for family and an occasional grocery clerk.

In my mind I'd arrived.

Battle scarred from messy dealings with humans, I was ready to settle in to the flexible, quiet life of being an entrepreneur and running a web and graphic design business helping local clients. It was a very good gig. But God may have been snickering at me as I thanked him for solitude that day. Turns out He had other plans for me.

My first novel idea struck me like a lightning bolt two years later. I was driving down the road with my 18-month-old daughter in the back seat and six months pregnant, this time with my son. I passed a sweetgrass basket maker at her stand on the side of the road and could "feel" her feeling invisible as my car kicked up dust and sped by. The story hit me with such sudden force that I grabbed a receipt and a pen and started writing the idea for *The Spirit of Sweetgrass* on the car console.

I went home and told my husband I had a great idea for a novel. He looked at me, not sure how to respond to his pregnant wife, and said, "That's nice, honey." This was not a suitable response for the magnitude of what had just happened to me. Not even close. So I hit the computer that night and started researching sweetgrass basket making in the Lowcountry and New Orleans voodoo.

The next morning I awoke at 4:00 and slipped down to my home office. I could almost hear my character telling me her tale. I wasn't sure what was happening, I simply knew I had to pen this story.

After a couple of weeks of writing, I decided to share my work with my husband or my mother, or both. Each was an unreliable source at this point. My mother loves me, and I figured she'd tell me what I wanted to hear. Ditto with my husband. It was then I discovered my church had a community group for writers that met at the local Barnes and Noble every other Tuesday. I was so hesitant to venture outside comfort, but I decided I had to take a chance for the sake of my story. One night I waddled in to a meeting, quite pregnant and the youngest of the group by at least a couple decades. We huddled around tables in the café and each read a short poem or chapter or whatnot for critique.

And they liked my book. This vulnerable group of mostly 60-, 70-, and 80-year-olds shared their most intimate writings with me and then encouraged me to continue mine. It's hard to explain the effect that had on me, a complete stranger who had entered the writing life quite unexpectedly. They blew fierce winds into my sails. I'd found my tribe.

One special soul, Red Evans, was in his seventies, a former radio DJ (the Rockin' Redhead) and TV news director, he'd had a varied life working in Charleston and also in Washington, D.C., as a congressional aide and lobbyist. He'd completed books and even had an agent. I looked up to him as the wise one who knew much more than me about writing and publishing. He kept trimmed bonsai trees in his dining room and spoke lovingly of his "bride" Marie. And that deep, resonant voice, I can still hear it. He had a diplomatic way of encouraging me in critiques without crushing my spirit. He had written a novel about a panther in the Carolinas and another about dog fighting, but neither had been published. He was currently writing a novel about a 12-year-old boy. When his fiddler friend dies on the farm next door, an old bandmate takes him on the ride of his life down to New Orleans to bury the fiddler near his first love—in a pickup truck with the body in the back on a kiddie pool of ice.

Irene Nuite Lofton was our poet. She was in her eighties, which was nothing because her mother was still alive, well over 100 years old. Irene wore coke-bottle glasses and was legally blind but saw well enough to plunk out stunning poetry on her keyboard. She wrote of hurricanes and old mill wheels, of hope after loss. She was practically triple my age but spoke of not yet being spiritually mature enough to attempt contemplative poetry. She had a friend she spoke to by phone every day. Between the two of them, they covered family and friends with prayer daily. Irene did things by hand, the old-fashioned way. As time went on, each new book of mine brought a handwritten note by Irene, telling me how proud she and the rest of the gang were of me.

Fred Robinson was in his seventies. He picked up Irene and brought her to the bookstore every other Tuesday. He'd also printed, hand-bound, and published chapbooks of Irene's poetry over the years. Fred was working on a science fiction novel. Formerly, he'd worked at the old naval base in Charleston and brought quirky engineer-type characters into his book. He got such a kick out of the antics his characters got into that he'd crack up and wipe his eyes reading them. At a party at his house one time around the pool, he offered me some of his homemade elderberry wine. A hand-built outhouse perched in the backyard.

I was in my early thirties, and these became my closest friends. They accepted me and understood intimately the writer part of me. Writers are not like other people. We have worlds going on in our heads. We are compelled to get them out on the page. It's not convenient and very rarely looks sane. Writer friends understand this deep dilemma. My friends validated that deepest part of me.

When my first novel was published, I was invited to speak to the Gullah Geechee Nation at their annual meeting held at the local library. My main character, Essie Mae, was of the same heritage, a basket maker who sat on the side of the road making baskets that actually affected the lives of her customers. I will admit I was a bit intimidated speaking on a topic I'd recently learned about to a group of people who lived it every day. I looked out over a sea of faces and there, two little specks, sat my mother and Fred, with that handsome glint in his eye. Seeing him gave me courage. So when Queen Quet cut me off while I was reading my character in dialect, I slung my tail between my legs, but stood tall because Fred had come out of his way to support me.

The Spirit of Sweetgrass, my debut novel, was released in March 2007. My friend Red's book, *On Ice*, about the fiddler, was published six months later in September. It was his debut, too, something he'd worked toward for years, but this was a bittersweet victory. That summer, Red found out he had stomach cancer. He seemed to get his best and worst news all at once. A grand book launch was planned at our meeting place, the Barnes and Noble. He had his barbershop buddies serenade the audience. He read from his book, and not a dry eye remained. We all knew it was also his going-away party.

By December Red entered the hospital. I needed more time with him, and so I visited him often over the next forty days. On once such occasion, I rode the elevator up with his son, who looked more than shocked. I asked if he was doing okay. He replied, "I just won the lottery." Yes, on the way to visit his dying father, he'd won the lottery, how much, I can't remember. But the irony wasn't lost. It was much like Red, selling his novel only to find out he had terminal cancer.

One day in the hospital, Red and I were chatting as he lay in bed. We spoke of the "old days" when I first began to come to our writing group and how everyone's words seemed to fly out of their fingertips. It was magical, simply put, the joining of writer souls together. I told Red it was as if the Holy Spirit had met us there. He agreed and then said, "It's not there anymore." He was right. Whatever it was in the beginning, whatever it was that brought us together and fueled us all, had slowly crept away with talk of publishing and dying. Then Red told me that the most important thing he had ever done was to write that novel. I had a hard time with this. Really? He'd done many important things. "Why?" I asked him.

"Because it showed my children who I really was."

In Red's dying days, he saw that sharing his true self with his family was the most important thing in life. I was humbled by his truth. "If you give a boy a fiddle and he doesn't play it, it's an abomination," he said. Whether it was the morphine or God speaking through him I'll never know. But I know one thing. I made Red a promise that day to "always keep writing." On days, months, years, when I don't know if I'll ever have another good word to write, I remember my promise to him to use my gift. It was his dying wish for me—one I intend to keep.

Red, Fred, and Irene have each since passed away. I didn't know how short our time would be together, and yet, they live on.

Five years ago, my husband and I made the choice to sell our home and move the kids to a new neighborhood and a new school. I was so anxious about it all, and one day in particular prayed on the way home. "Lord, I'm changing everything for my kids. Everything!"

My car pulled in to the drive, and I checked the mailbox. There was a large envelope addressed to me from a stranger. Upon further inspection, it was from a friend of Irene's, one I'd met at her funeral. "Dear Nicole," it read. She explained that she was tasked with going through Irene's belongings. She'd run across something that seemed very important to Irene and wanted me to have it. There before my eyes was a first chapter of a middle grade novel I once wrote and shared with my writers' group. The title? *The Boy Who Changed Everything.*

Changing everything. It was as if a handwritten note of encouragement from Irene fell from heaven. As if she was up there, pulling strings and letting me know that everything was going to be all right with the move. That gave me such needed peace, it's hard to describe or fathom.

Writer friendships are not normal, nor would we want them to be. Look at Lewis and Tolkien. Iron sharpens iron. Knowing the value of writer friends who also share my faith, a few years ago after considering giving up writing altogether, I knew I needed to find a new tribe. I put out a call and wound up meeting every other week with two local published authors, Dianne Miley and Dorothy McFalls. We were each in waiting rooms of life with regard to writing. I was switching genres and working on an intense historical novel with research that threatened to pull me under. Dorothy was pregnant and then with a new child, a change that alters everything. And Dianne was looking to leave her job and begin volunteering at a local crisis pregnancy center, both as philanthropy and as research for a new novel. We met, had coffee, shared our lives, talked about books, shared Bible verses, and prayed. It was Dianne who, when I begged her to give me a real deadline so I could actually get something completed, gave me till the end of the summer.

Her deadline, her firmness, was exactly what I needed. She knew that. She's a writer. Though life is getting busier and we meet once every few months now, I'm so grateful to know these friendships will be a constant through the ups and downs of my writing future.

In saving this final friend for last, it is only that I'm not sure how to describe the importance of her friendship to me. We call each other "thin friends," and although I'd love it to describe our appearances, it's really about our spiritual connection. In Irish lore, "thin places" are where the spiritual envelope is pierced and a bit of heaven comes through into the real world. That's what happens whenever I speak to author Shellie Rushing Tomlinson. She lives in Louisiana, several states away from my South Carolina, but when we speak, we each enter a mystical "thin place." We encounter empathy and prophecy, encouragement and inspiration. Our minds whir with ideas, and we can hardly keep up with what the Lord does between us as it all spills out. It's the kind of conversation in which one should take notes because monumental shifts occur—book ideas, titles, scripture revelations, the state of our world, honesty, honesty, and more honesty. Our chatter could fill the pages of a book and may very well have to do that someday.

I met Shellie at a Pulpwood Queens Girlfriends Weekend in Jefferson, Texas. This is an annual meeting for the largest and wildest book club in the country. She was dressed as a rainbow. I think I was wearing wings. A costume party raged around us, and for a moment, we needed some peace and quiet, so we each found our way into the authors' room. We were the only two in there. We spoke and connected instantly, nearly had church right there. Not coincidentally, we were only a couple of the people there not drinking that night, so we were more than clearheaded. Each of us was fasting—she with her church in Louisiana, and me with mine in South Carolina.

Shellie is the Belle of All Things Southern and has a radio show to match. She's also a humorist (blurbed by Jeff Foxworthy) and a Jesus-loving devotional and cookbook author who rubs shoulders with the Duck Dynasty gang in Monroe, Louisiana. Needless to say, when I tell my family I'm going off to go talk to Shellie on the phone (meaning, don't bother me for a while), they say, "Oh boy, she's about to start talking really loud and really southern." Why yes, I am. A southern soul sister can truly bring out the best in you!

I met a true sister of my soul that night in Jefferson, one who has cried and laughed with me. I trust Shellie with my heart and dreams. I called her literally as my dog Kahlua lay dying in my arms. In those moments I wanted her to pray with me. I wanted my thin place friend to help me pierce that membrane between heaven and earth. To this day, just the thought of her cheers me up and urges me to get writing again. Because she knows how important it is—writing is part of the reason we're here. Like most southerners, we each understand there are voices in our heads, but good ones, we're convinced. We're just tasked with getting them out on paper.

And now, all this talk about writer friends has made me nostalgic. Some of my friends are gone from the earth but live on my heart and mind. Others are just a phone call or coffee away. But as I develop more and more into someone-who-must-write, I find that I need these kindred spirits with me, keeping me on track. For my friends I say a familiar prayer of gratitude: *Lord, thank you for understanding me. For giving me peace.*

Writing is a solitary affair and very often done by introverts. And yet the publishing business demands we be extroverts, a dilemma indeed. It's enough to make one consider another career. Except that being a writer isn't a career, it's closer to the color of your skin. We can't change it. As southern literary son Pat Conroy told me once, "If you gotta do it, you gotta do it."

To any writer out there I would say this: *Always know who your true writer friends are, the ones who really wish you well, who want what's best for you as much as they would for themselves, those who will both celebrate your successes and grieve at your failures.* They will never be jealous and will lift you up when you drag yourself, limping along. They're not everywhere, but they're out there. Find them!

How can I have been so blessed to have such special writer friends touch my soul? Perhaps it's just a willingness to stick my neck out there, or perhaps it's because my community here in Charleston is so supportive of writers. At every turn, a new book, novel, or cookbook is released here and one might be honored with an invitation to the home of our southern culinary grand dame, Nathalie Dupree, or our beloved conservation-minded novelist Mary Alice Monroe, or even our Poet Laureate Marjory Wentworth. Perhaps you're in Beaufort, S.C., where the new Pat Conroy Literary Center carries on his legacy of breathing life into our southern literary world. Or maybe there's some special hub for writers in your neck of the woods. If you get an invitation to be around writers, get out of your PJs, leave your writing desk, and go. You may find yourself rubbing shoulders with a writer who shares something deeply in common with you and needs a shoulder to lean on. Strike up a conversation with him or her. Don't be afraid. We're all introverts wearing extroverted lives.

In this topsy-turvy game of the writer's life and publishing world, there will come a time when you have to put it all on the line and phone a friend . . . for sanity, for direction, for prayer. Make sure you've got a good one in your corner.

Keep Truckin'

Michael Farris Smith

I did a brief stint in Oxford, Mississippi, back when I was a younger man and in the middle of the drift of early adulthood, though the earliness of it was wearing off fast. I lived a half block off the Square in a big house divided up into apartments, right across the street from the original office of the *Oxford American*. One evening I walked over to Square Books, my first venture into the legendary bookstore, and on the front table I found a story collection called *Big Bad Love*, and a novella titled *Ray*. I picked each of them up because they were on the table of "Mississippi Writers." This was my introduction to both Larry Brown and Barry Hannah, and little did I know what that moment would mean to me.

I walked back to my apartment and up the stairs and I went out and sat on the shared porch. The porch light was faint but was good for reading, so I decided to read the first story in *Big Bad Love*. But by the time I left the porch that night, whatever time that was, I had devoured both books. Inhaled them. Loved them and immediately loved the writers who had written with such striking, beautiful prose. I remember that what kept occurring to me as I read was the notion that I knew the people they were writing about. I knew those winding, dark, bumpy back roads. I knew the dimly lit bars and cheap brands of bourbon and the feelings of loneliness and wonder that these characters were experiencing.

My few months in Oxford came in the midst of living abroad for a few years and it was only recently that I had become a reader. And I had become a reader simply out of necessity to fill the hours in my Geneva apartment, or to pass the time on the train or sitting in the cafes or the park. I was inexperienced as a reader, so most of what I had read were the big names because they were the only names I knew. Hemingway, Faulkner, Dickens, Fitzgerald. And with Hemingway and Fitzgerald I found connections in their stories of the Left Bank or southern Spain because those were the places I was experiencing then. But when I met the stories of Larry Brown and Barry Hannah, I realized what it meant to be a southern writer in the here and now. I knew their Mississippi firsthand and it shook me. I remember packing their work with me when I went back to Geneva and reading it again and again.

What I didn't know, but now realize, is that was the beginnings of my becoming a writer. I didn't start writing for another couple of years, but that feeling was in me. From reading interviews with Brown and Hannah I then discovered writers like William Gay, Richard Yates, and Harry Crews, and those writers and their stories got into me and were not to let go. And the more I read, the more I found in myself.

So a couple of years later when the time came for me to come back to the States, I made one of those kinds of decisions that only the person making it can understand. I'm going back to Mississippi, I decided. And I'm going to try and become a writer.

⟡

If only it were that easy.

I published a handful of stories in literary journals and reviews over the next few years and felt like I was on the edge of breaking through, and I knew that would only come with a novel. I turned my attention to the longer form and discovered I liked it. I enjoyed being with my characters for a longer amount of time, getting to know them more thoroughly, thinking of a story in a bigger way. Like every other person who has ever written fiction, I stopped and started a few different things, tossed out some pages, held on to others, and kept trying to get better.

And then I finally did. I wrote a novella called *The Hands of Strangers* and I could tell that it felt different. I could feel my voice mature in the storytelling. I believed I had something that was good, or maybe a little better. So I began to submit it to agents and a few editors and they all seemed to agree with me. It's good, and maybe even better than good. But . . .

No one was going to publish a novella by a first-time author. That's what the agents said. And the editors said there is no way I can get my boss to publish this novella with it being your first book. All the work, all the frustrations, all the rejection I had received up until then felt like no pain at all compared to being told this is a helluva piece of work but because of things other than the work itself, we are passing.

I kept trying with it for a couple of years, all the while continuing to write stories and waiting for a novel idea to come along, and nothing happened. And then I gave up submitting it. Stuck it in the file and left it to be. The words of writers like Brown and Gay and Crews rattled around in my head, when they talked about their own experiences with rejection and the years of the apprenticeship that seemingly had no end. I wanted to quit and even promised myself on a few occasions that I was going to, but now it wasn't the fiction of the writers I admired that was keeping me going, but their own tales of perseverance. I finally shook it off, came around, and began to write a novel about the Mississippi Gulf Coast after years of being devastated by one hurricane after another, and I found that the work itself kept away the anxiety of failures, past and present. My confidence returned, my voice continued to mature, and it wasn't long before I had a couple of hundred pages of the novel that would become *Rivers,* and it was time to start writing those query letters again.

And nothing happened.

The four or five agents who liked *The Hands of Strangers* weren't interested in all the storms. Neither were the editors. But I have a novel now to go with the novella, I said. And it's a damn good novel, I said, not really knowing if it would end up that way or not. But nothing. Still, I rolled up my sleeves and finished a first draft of *Rivers,* because I had come too far not to.

⁌

It was August, and I sat on the back porch of our old Victorian with my wife. She was six months pregnant with our second daughter. School was about to start again. And I was about as low as I had ever been. She had picked me up time after time, but I think even she could tell this was different.

I'm done, I said. I'm going to give it until then end of this school year, next spring, and if nothing has happened, then I'm going to move on to whatever comes next. I'll keep submitting for the next nine months but that's it. There's no sense in me trying to write anything new with the baby about to be here anyway. She nodded and said if that's what you want to do. It is, I told her. I'm sure. I don't know whether she believed me or not. Then we managed to change the subject. In my mind, it was already over.

Three weeks later I got an email from the editor at a small press in Charlotte, North Carolina. He said that he was looking back through some older emails and ran across my submission of *The Hands of Strangers* from earlier in the year and he apologized for missing it. He had given the novella to one of his readers and despite the fact the decisions for their list had already been made, both he and the reader were impressed by it and would like to add it to their lineup for the spring. That is, if it's still available.

I was at home alone. I got up from the computer and walked outside and to the back porch. I sat down in the same spot where I had told my wife this is all over. And I was right, just not in the way I suspected. It was over. The waiting had ended.

Seven months later, the novella was published and received a starred review from *Publishers Weekly*, the only starred review ever received by the press, and only a few months after that, it took my revised *Rivers* only nine days from submission to sale in New York.

⌖

There is no trick. There is no magic. There is no shortcut. I read this in interviews with Hemingway, Brown, Carver, Crews, and many others. I believed it when I was struggling to both create and publish fiction and I believe it now that I have an agent and an editor and a publicist and an audience and so forth and so on. I believe you have to want it like nothing else and sometimes even that isn't enough. When I began, I had no idea what it was going to take. And I'm glad I didn't.

But I look back now at the night I walked into Square Books. I look back at my quiet nights in my Geneva apartment when I began to read. I look back at the handful of friends who encouraged me. I look back at the email I sent to the editor at the small press in North Carolina, in the middle of the night, when I couldn't sleep, when another baby was on the way, when I wanted to be able to tell my children you can do anything you want and believe it, and I see the pieces of my writing life fitting together. I couldn't see it then. No one can. And through all the rejection and frustration, one thing remained constant. I kept writing. I kept working. There is no substitute. You have to do the work and believe in yourself when no one else does.

You have to keep truckin'.

Contributors

JULIE CANTRELL is the *New York Times* and *USA Today* best-selling author of *Into the Free*, a debut novel that earned a starred review by *Publishers Weekly*, the Mississippi Library Association's Fiction Award, and the Christy Award Book of the Year while being named a Best Read of 2012 by *USA Today*. The sequel, *When Mountains Move*, was named a 2013 Best Read and won the Carol Award for Historical Fiction. Her third novel, *The Feathered Bone*, was selected as an Okra Pick by SIBA and Book of the Year by Pulpwood Queens. It earned a starred review by *Library Journal*, who also named it a Top Pick of 2016. Cantrell has served as editor-in-chief of the *Southern Literary Review* and is a recipient of the Mississippi Arts Commission Literary Fellowship as well as the Mary Elizabeth Nelson Fellowship at Rivendell Writers' Colony. Her fourth novel, *Perennials*, was released in November 2017. www.juliecantrell.com

KATHERINE CLARK is a native of Birmingham, Alabama, and a graduate of Harvard. She earned a PhD in American Literature from Emory with a dissertation on William Faulkner. She is the co-author of two oral biographies: *Motherwit: An Alabama Midwife's Story*, with Onnie Lee Logan, which was a *New York Times* Notable Book; and *Milking the Moon: A Southerner's Story of Life on this Planet*, with Eugene Walter, which was a finalist for a National Book Critics Circle award. Her series of Mountain Brook novels is being published by Pat Conroy's Story River Books imprint at the University of South Carolina Press. *The Headmaster's Darlings*, the first novel in this series, was the winner of the 2015 Willie Morris Award for Southern Fiction. *All the Governor's Men* and *The Harvard Bride* came out in 2016, followed by *The Ex-Suicide* in 2017. All four novels were awarded the Excellence in Writing award by the Fitzgerald Museum. She has recently completed an oral biography of the late great author Pat Conroy.

SUSAN CUSHMAN (editor) was co-director of the 2010 and 2013 Creative Nonfiction Conferences in Oxford, Mississippi, and director of the 2011 Memphis Creative Nonfiction Workshop. She is author of a novel, *Cherry Bomb* (August 2017), and a nonfiction book, *Tangles and Plaques: A Mother and Daughter Face Alzheimer's* (February 2017), and editor of *A Second Blooming: Becoming the Women We Are Meant to Be* (March 2017). Her essays have appeared in three anthologies and numerous journals and magazines. A native of Jackson, Mississippi, she lives in Memphis.

JIM DEES is the author of *The Statue and the Fury: A Year of Art, Race, Music and Cocktails*. Since 2000, he has been the host of the *Thacker Mountain Radio Hour*, a music and literature program heard weekly on Mississippi Public Broadcasting. He is also the author of *Lies and Other Truths*, a collection of his newspaper columns, and the editor of *They Write Among Us*, an anthology of Oxford writers. Dees lives in Lafayette County, Mississippi.

CLYDE EDGERTON is the author of ten novels and two books of nonfiction. He is the Thomas S. Kenan Distinguished Professor of Creative Writing at the University of North Carolina Wilmington.

W. RALPH EUBANKS is the author of *Ever Is a Long Time: A Journey Into Mississippi's Dark Past* and *The House at the End of the Road: The Story of Three Generations of an Interracial Family in the American South*. A 2007 Guggenheim fellow, his essays and criticism have appeared in the *Washington Post*, the *Wall Street Journal*, NPR, *WIRED*, and the *New Yorker*. He lives with his family in Washington, D.C.

JOHN M. FLOYD's work has appeared in more than 250 different publications, including *Alfred Hitchcock Mystery Magazine*, *Ellery Queen Mystery Magazine*, *The Strand Magazine*, the *Saturday Evening Post*, *Writer's Digest*, *Mississippi Noir*, and *The Best American Mystery Stories 2015*. A former Air Force captain and IBM systems engineer, John is also a three-time Derringer Award winner and an Edgar Award nominee. His sixth book, *Dreamland*, was released in October 2016.

JOE FORMICHELLA, author of 2016's *Schopenhauer's Maxim: A Novel Conspiracy*, is a multiple literary award winner, including a Hackney Literary

Award (short fiction) and a 2008 *ForeWord* magazine nonfiction book of the year (*Murder Creek*). He was a finalist for a national IPPY Award for true crime (*Murder Creek*), a finalist for a New Letters Literary Prize, and a Pushcart Prize nominee whose short fiction has appeared in several reviews and anthologies. His recent work includes 2014's *Waffle House Rules*, a novel, and 2015's nonfiction *A Condition of Freedom*. He lives near Fairhope, Alabama, with his wife, author Suzanne Hudson. Contact joe_formichella@yahoo.com.

PATTI CALLAHAN HENRY is a *New York Times* best-selling author of twelve novels. Her latest is *The Bookshop at Water's End* (July 2017). She was a finalist for the Townsend Prize for Fiction, an Indie Next Pick on Okra Pick, and a multiple nominee for the Southern Independent Booksellers Alliance (SIBA) Novel of the Year. Her essays have appeared in *Southern Living*, *Birmingham Magazine*, *Writer's Digest*, and others. Patti attended Auburn University for her undergraduate work and Georgia State University for her graduate degree. Once a pediatric clinical nurse specialist, she now writes full time. The mother of three children, she lives in both Mountain Brook, Alabama, and Bluffton, South Carolina, with her husband. Visit her online at patticallahanhenry.com, facebook.com/AuthorPattiCallahanHenry, twitter. com/pcalhenry, and pinterest.com/patticalhenry.

Raised in Arkansas and a longtime resident of Alabama, JENNIFER HORNE is a writer, editor, and teacher who explores southern identity and experience, especially women's, through prose, poetry, fiction, and anthologies and in classrooms and workshops across the South. Among her books are *Bottle Tree: Poems* (2010) and *Tell the World You're a Wildflower* (2014), a collection of short stories in the voices of southern women and girls. Her new collection of road and travel poems, *Little Wanderer*, was published by Salmon Poetry in 2016, and she has co-edited, with Don Noble, a collection of short fiction by Alabama women, *Belles' Letters II* (2017). She is at work on a biography of writer Sara Mayfield. Horne was named Poet Laureate of Alabama in 2017.

RAVI HOWARD is the author of two books of fiction, *Like Trees, Walking* (HarperCollins, 2007) and *Driving the King* (HarperCollins, 2015). He has received fellowships and awards from the New Jersey Council on the Arts, the Hurston-Wright Foundation, Bread Loaf Writers' Conference, and the National Endowment for the Arts. In addition to being selected as a finalist for the Hemingway Foundation/PEN Award, *Like Trees, Walking*, his first novel, won the Ernest J. Gaines Award for Literary Excellence (2008). He is also a professor of creative writing at Florida State University.

SUZANNE HUDSON's first short story collection, *Opposable Thumbs*, was a finalist for a John Gardner Fiction Book Award in 2001. She has since had short stories in *Stories from the Blue Moon Café*, volumes I, II, and IV, *The Alumni Grill*, *Climbing Mt. Cheaha*, *A Kudzu Christmas*, *State of Laughter*, *Men Undressed: Women Writers on the Male Sexual Experience*, *Delta Blues*, and *The Shoe Burnin': Stories of Southern Soul*. A second short fiction collection, *All the Way to Memphis*, came out in 2014. Her first novel, *In a Temple of Trees*, was rereleased in August 2017); her second novel, *In the Dark of the Moon*, was rereleased in 2016. A fictional memoir, *Second Sluthood*, Second E-dition, and a novel, *The Fall of the Nixon Administration*, are due out in 2018. Hudson lives near Fairhope, Alabama, on Waterhole Branch with her husband, author Joe Formichella.

RIVER JORDAN is a southerner with a global perspective. She began her writing career as a playwright and spent over ten years in the theatre both writing and directing. She went on to become a best-selling author and her work has been most frequently cast in the company of such authors as O'Connor, Faulkner, and Harper Lee. Her novels include *The Gin Girl*, *The Messenger of Magnolia Street*, *Saints in Limbo*, and *The Miracle of Mercy Land*. Her nonfiction memoir, *Praying for Strangers: An Adventure of the Human Spirit*, ushered in a movement that continues to inspire and change lives. Ms. Jordan teaches and speaks around the country on the power of story in our lives. She spent eight years producing and hosting her radio program *Clearstory*, which is broadcast in Nashville, and is at work developing the podcast. In the fullness of time, *Confessions of an American Mystic* (Jericho Books, Hachette) will arrive in bookstores everywhere. Ms. Jordan lives with her furry beasts in Nashville.

HARRISON SCOTT KEY is the author of *The World's Largest Man*, winner of the 2016 Thurber Prize in American Humor. His nonfiction and humor have appeared in the *New York Times*, *Outside*, *McSweeney's Internet Tendency*, *The Best American Travel Writing*, *Southern Living*, *Salon*, *Reader's Digest*, *Image*, *Creative Nonfiction*, *Gulf Coast*, and the *Oxford American*, where he serves as a contributing editor. He teaches writing at the Savannah College of Art and Design in Savannah, Georgia, where he lives with his wife and three children. Online, you can find him at www.HarrisonScottKey.com and www. facebook.com/harrisonscottkey. On Twitter, he's @HarrisonKey.

CASSANDRA KING, author of five novels, a book of nonfiction, numerous short stories, magazine articles, and essays, is a native of L.A. (Lower Alabama). Her first novel, *Making Waves*, has been through numerous printings since its release in 1995. Her *USA Today* and *New York Times* best-selling second novel, *The Sunday Wife*, was a *People* magazine Page-Turner, a South Carolina's Readers Circle choice, named as one of *Book Sense*'s top reading group selections, and chosen by the Nestle Corporation for a national campaign promoting reading groups. *The Same Sweet Girls*, also a *New York Times* best-seller, was a number one *Book Sense* selection on release. Both novels were nominated for SIBA's Book of the Year award. *Moonrise* was a SIBA Okra Pick and best-seller, as was *The Same Sweet Girls Guide to Life*: *Advice from a Failed Southern Belle*. She resides in the low country of South Carolina, and is currently working on a memoir/cookbook.

ALAN LIGHTMAN is an American writer, physicist, and social entrepreneur. Lightman has served on the faculties of Harvard and the Massachusetts Institute of Technology (MIT) and is currently professor of the practice of the humanities at MIT. He has a PhD in physics from the California Institute of Technology and has received five honorary doctoral degrees. His essays and articles have appeared in the *Atlantic, Granta, Harper's,* the *New Yorker,* the *New York Review of Books, Salon,* and many other publications. His six novels include *Einstein's Dreams*, an international best-seller, and *The Diagnosis,* a finalist for the National Book Award. He is also the author of a number of nonfiction books, including *Screening Room*, a memoir of the South, and *The Accidental Universe*. In 2005 he founded the Harpswell Foundation, whose mission is to empower a new generation of women leaders in Cambodia.

SONJA LIVINGSTON's most recent book, *Ladies Night at the Dreamland,* combines history, memory, and imagination to explore the lives of women from America's recent and distant past. She's the author of a recent essay collection, *Queen of the Fall,* and a memoir, *Ghostbread,* winner of the AWP Award in Nonfiction. Her work has won a NFYA Nonfiction Fellowship, an

Iowa Review Award, the Susan Atefat Essay Prize, and grants from Vermont Studio Center and the Deming Fund for Women. Sonja teaches in the Creative Writing Program at Virginia Commonwealth University.

COREY MESLER has been published in numerous anthologies and journals including *Poetry, Gargoyle, Five Points, Good Poems, American Places*, and *Esquire/Narrative*. He has published nine novels, four short story collections, and five full-length poetry collections. He has been nominated for the Pushcart many times, and two of his poems were chosen for Garrison Keillor's Writer's Almanac. With his wife he runs a 140-year-old bookstore in Memphis. He can be found at https://coreymesler.wordpress.com.

NILES REDDICK's newest novel *Drifting Too Far From the Shore* has been nominated for a Pulitzer. Previously, his collection *Road Kill Art and Other Oddities* was a finalist for an Eppie award, and his first novella *Lead Me Home* was a national finalist for a *ForeWord* magazine award. His work has appeared in anthologies *Southern Voices in Every Direction, Unusual Circumstances, Getting Old*, and *Happy Holidays*. Author of nearly one hundred stories, Reddick has been featured in many literary magazines and journals including the *Arkansas Review: A Journal of Delta Studies, Southern Reader, Like the Dew*, the *Dead Mule School of Southern Literature*, the *Pomanok Review, Corner Club Press, Slice of Life, Faircloth Review*, and many others. Reddick works for the University of Memphis, Lambuth, in Jackson, Tennessee. His website is www.nilesreddick.com.

WENDY REED is an Emmy-winning public TV producer and writer. She produces for two series at the University of Alabama (*Bookmark with Don Noble* and *Discovering Alabama*), where she teaches science and nature writing in the Honors College. In addition to publishing stories and essays, she has written *An Accidental Memoir* and co-edited two collections with Jennifer Horne, *Circling Faith* and *All Out of Faith*. The Alabama State Council on the Arts fellow lives with her husband in Hoover and is at work on a book about the short, tragic life of southern writer Clarence Cason.

NICOLE SEITZ is the author of six highly acclaimed novels: *Beyond Molasses Creek, The Inheritance of Beauty, Saving Cicadas, A Hundred Years of Happiness, Trouble the Water*, and *The Spirit of Sweetgrass*. Most recently, she edited *When You Pass through Waters: Words of Hope and Healing from Your Favorite Authors* for flood relief. Seitz holds a BA in journalism from the University of North Carolina–Chapel Hill and a BFA in illustration from Savannah College of Art and Design. She lives in Charleston, South Carolina, where she teaches art and summer workshops for creative writing and illustration. Her seventh novel, *The Cage-maker*, was released in August 2017 from University of South Carolina Press.

LEE SMITH began writing stories at the age of nine and selling them for a nickel apiece. Since then, she has written seventeen works of fiction, including *Fair and Tender Ladies*, *Oral History*, and most recently, *Guests on Earth*. She has received numerous awards, including the North Carolina Award for Literature and an Academy Award in Fiction from the American Academy of Arts and Letters; her novel *The Last Girls* was a *New York Times* best-seller as well as winner of the Southern Book Critics Circle Award. She lives in Hillsborough, North Carolina, with her husband, the writer Hal Crowther.

MICHAEL FARRIS SMITH is the award-winning author of several novels, including *Desperation Road* (a Barnes & Noble Discover pick and an Indie Next selection), *Rivers* (for which he received the Mississippi Author Award for Fiction), and *The Hands of Strangers*. He has been awarded the Mississippi Arts Commission Literary Arts Fellowship, the Transatlantic Review Award for Fiction, and the Alabama Arts Council Fellowship Award for Literature. His short fiction has twice been nominated for a Pushcart Prize, and his essays have appeared in the *New York Times*, *Catfish Alley*, *Deep South* magazine, and more. He lives in Oxford, Mississippi, with his wife and two daughters.

SALLY PALMER THOMASON, born and raised in California, attended Occidental College and the International Graduate School of the University of Stockholm. Having lived in Memphis since the mid-1950s, she taught history at St. Mary's Episcopal School and was dean of lifelong learning at Rhodes College, where she developed interdisciplinary programs in the humanities and social sciences. After earning a PhD from the Union Institute and University when she was in her sixties, she taught courses on holistic aging at the Memphis Theological Seminary and has continued to explore the ways culture shapes an individual's beliefs and values in the three books she has written: *The Living Spirit of the Crone: Turning Aging Inside Out*, *The Topaz Brooch*, and *Delta Rainbow: The Irrepressible Betty Bobo Pearson* (University Press of Mississippi, 2016). Sally and her husband John have three grown children and four grandchildren.

JACQUELINE ALLEN TRIMBLE, PhD, lives and writes in Montgomery, Alabama, where she is the chairperson of Languages and Literatures at Alabama State University. Her work has appeared in *The Offing*, *Blue Lake Review*, and *The Griot*. Her poetry collection, *American Happiness*, is published by NewSouth Books. Recently awarded a Key West Literary Seminar scholarship, she is currently the recipient of a 2017 literary arts fellowship from the Alabama State Council on the Arts. *American Happiness* was chosen as the poetry finalist and named Seven Sisters Book Award Best Book of 2016.

M. O. WALSH is from Baton Rouge, Louisiana. He is the author of the story collection *The Prospect of Magic* and the novel *My Sunshine Away*, which was a *New York Times* best-seller and winner of the Pat Conroy Book Award for general fiction. He teaches at the University of New Orleans.

CLAUDE WILKINSON is a critic, essayist, painter, and poet. His criticism has explored such diverse artists and authors as photographers Maude Schuyler Clay and James Van Der Zee, fiction writers Chinua Achebe, John Cheever, and Flannery O'Connor, playwright Charles Fuller, and poet Etheridge Knight, among others. His poetry collections include *Reading the Earth*, winner of the Naomi Long Madgett Poetry Award, and *Joy in the Morning*, which was nominated for a Pulitzer Prize. Other honors include a Whiting Writers' Award and the W. M. Whittington Jr. Purchase Award for painting.

Index